Straightforward

Beginner Student's Book

MACMILLAN

CONTENTS

	Pronunciation	Reading	Listening	Speaking
1A	Contractions (1)	Dialogues: four greetings		Meet other students
1B			Introductions	Dialogue: introductions
1C	Intonation (1) (*wh-* questions)		Four phone dialogues	Roleplay: phone numbers
1D				
2A	The alphabet		At the hotel	At the hotel
2B		Dialogue: in a hotel room		Asking what something is in English
2C	/iː/		In a café	Roleplay: in a café
2D				
3A	Consonants: /dʒ/, /d/, /r/ & /tʃ/	*International workers*		Communication: jobs
3B	Contractions (2)		Dialogue on a train	Game: *Correct or incorrect?*
3C		*United Nations International School*		
3D				
4A	Word stress (1)		Dialogues about age	Talking about how old things are
4B	Schwa /ə/	Family album web page		Talking about your family
4C			In a flat	Communication: describe and draw
4D				
5A		*Working life*		Talk about where you live and work
5B	Consonants: /s/ & /z/		Dialogues about technology	*Technology Life Survey*
5C	Intonation (2): (*yes/no* questions)	Interview with a man about his new job		Game: *My new job – a hard life?*
5D				
6A	/e/, /ʌ/, /uː/ & /ɪ/	*Morning people and night people*		Talking about your daily routine
6B	Connected speech (1)	Community centre noticeboard	Phone call to a community centre	Roleplay: a famous person's free time
6C		*Eating habits survey*		Make a healthy living survey
6D				

	Pronunciation	Reading	Listening	Speaking
7A	Word stress (2)	*Take a break in the world's top cities*		Presentation: a city you know
7B		Dialogue about a neighbourhood		Communication: Two places
7C	/m/, /f/, /v/ & /p/		In the city of York	Roleplay: tourists in New York
7D				
8A	Years	*Do it again*		Talking about films and TV Presentation about you in the past
8B		Dialogue from a detective film		*Find someone who …*
8C	Intonation (3)		Dialogues about opinions	Game: *That's My Opinion*
8D				
9A		Email about a holiday		Talk about a real or imaginary place you went on holiday
9B	Past simple regular verbs	The Beatles' last concert		Retell the story of the Beatles
9C	/θ/ & /ð/		Independence day holidays	Interview about independence day holidays
9D				
10A	Diphthongs		Dialogue about the weekend	Guided dialogue about the week-end
10B	Connected speech (2)	Quizzes in Britain	A quiz	Make a quiz
10C		*Night markets – the place for a good deal*	In a shop	Shopping questionnaire Roleplay: in a shop
10D				
11A	*Can/can't*	*People look at us*		Game: *The English Challenge!*
11B	/ŋ/		At a concert	Dialogues on the phone
11C		*Special paintings*	Dialogues about paintings	Describe a painting
11D				
12A	Intonation (4)	*Me and my mobile*	Three phone calls	Guided phone call
12B			At the airport	Describe a picture Roleplay: at the airport
12C	*Going to*	*The end of the course!*		Guided dialogue – end of course
12D				

1A | My name

Grammar: *To be* (1); *I am*; *What is your name? My name is …*
Vocabulary: Names
Functional language: Greetings (1); Asking & saying names

A

FUNCTIONAL LANGUAGE: greetings (1)

1 1.1 Read and listen.

Hello.
Hi. Goodbye.
Bye.

2 1.1 Listen again and repeat.

3 Say *hello* to other people in the class.

B

READING & LISTENING

1 1.2 Listen to the dialogues and point to the correct photo.

2 1.2 Listen again and read the dialogues.

1
A: Hello.
B: Hi.
A: What's your name?
B: My name's Jack.

2
A: Goodbye.
B: Goodbye.

3
A: Hi.
B: Hello.
A: I'm … Orion. What's your name?
B: My name's Emily.

4
A: What's your name?
B: Willy.
A: Goodbye, Willy.

C

D

FUNCTIONAL LANGUAGE: asking & saying names

1 1.3 Listen and repeat.

A: What's your name?
B: My name's Ben. What's yours?
A: I'm Emma.

2 Work in pairs. Ask and say your name.

GRAMMAR: *to be* (1)

Full form		**Contraction**
I am	=	***I'm***
What is	=	***What's***
My name is	=	***My name's***

SEE LANGUAGE REFERENCE PAGE 22

1 Complete the dialogues with *'m* or *'s*.

1
A: Hello. What (1) _____ your name?
B: I (2) _____ Thomas.
A: Hello, Thomas.

2
A: I (3) _____ Mr Smith. What (4) _____ your name?
B: My name (5) _____ Jessica.
A: Goodbye, Jessica.
B: Bye.

2 1.4 Listen to the recording to check your answers.

PRONUNCIATION: contractions (1)

1 1.5 Listen and repeat.

I am	I'm
My name is	My name's
What is	What's

2 Practise the dialogues in Grammar exercise 1. Use contractions.

SPEAKING

1 Walk around the class and meet other students. Use the diagram to help you.

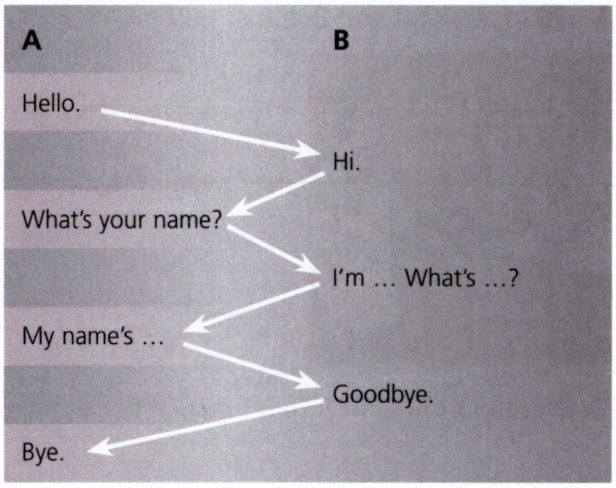

ENGLISH AROUND YOU: names

1 1.6 Listen to some popular names in Britain.

2 Do you know people with British names? If yes, what are they? Which British names are popular in your country?

1B My country

Grammar: *To be* (2) (*my, his, her*)
Vocabulary: Cities & countries
Functional language: Greetings (2); Asking & saying where you're from

FUNCTIONAL LANGUAGE: greetings (2)

1 1.7 Read and listen.

A: Hello, Lucy.
B: Hi, Dan. This is Philip.
A: Nice to meet you, Philip.
C: Nice to meet you, too.

2 Work in groups of three. Practise the dialogue.

VOCABULARY: cities & countries

1 Match the countries 1–8 to the photos A–H.

1 Brazil	5 France
2 Italy	6 the US
3 Britain	7 China
4 Russia	8 Germany

2 1.8 Listen to the recording to check your answers. Repeat the words.

LISTENING

1 1.9 Listen and write the names of the countries or cities you hear.

1 My name is Polly. I'm from ______.
2 This is Pierre. He's from ______, ______.
3 Her name's Sofia. She's from ______.
4 His name's Michael. He's from ______.
5 Where are you from?
We're from ______.
6 This is Nikita and Igor. They're from ______.

2 1.9 Listen again and repeat.

A Bejing

B Moscow

C New York

D Frankfurt

E Paris

F Rome

GRAMMAR: *to be* (2) (*my, his, her*)

Full form		Contraction
He **is**	=	*He***'s**
She **is**	=	*She***'s**
We **are**	=	*We***'re**
They **are**	=	*They***'re**

My *name is …*
His *name is …*
Her *name is …*

SEE LANGUAGE REFERENCE PAGE 22

1 Underline the correct form of the verb to complete the sentences.

1 I *am / are* Jennifer.
2 His name *is / are* George.
3 They *are / am* from England.
4 He *is / am* from London.
5 She *is / are* from Manchester.
6 We *are / is* from Russia.

2 Make sentences about the photos.

A *Her name is Jin.*
She's from China.

A Jin, China

B Edgar, Germany

C Julio, Brazil

D Jennifer, US

G London

FUNCTIONAL LANGUAGE: asking & saying where you're from

1 1.10 Read and listen.

A: Where are you from?
B: I'm from Milan.

2 Work in groups. Ask other students, *Where are you from?*

SPEAKING

1 Work in groups of three, A, B and C. Complete the dialogue with information about you.

A: Hi. I'm ______. What's your name?
B: Hello. My name's ______. I'm from ______. Where are you from?
A: I'm from ______.

A: Hello, ______.
C: Hi, ______.
A: This is ______. He/She's from ______.
C: Nice to meet you.
B: Nice to meet you, too.

2 Practise the dialogue.

3 Close your books and practise the dialogue again.

H Rio de Janeiro

1c My number

Grammar: *It*
Vocabulary: Numbers 1–10
Functional language: Greetings (3); Asking for & saying phone numbers

FUNCTIONAL LANGUAGE: greetings (3)

1 1.11 Read and listen.

A: Hello. How are you?
B: I'm fine, thanks. And you?
A: Fine, thanks.

2 1.11 Listen again and repeat.

3 Work in groups. Say hello to the other people. Ask, *How are you?* and answer.

VOCABULARY: numbers 1–10

1 1.12 Read and listen to the numbers.

2 1.13 Listen and say the correct number.

LISTENING

1 1.14 Listen to four dialogues. Match the dialogues 1–4 to the pictures A–D.

A
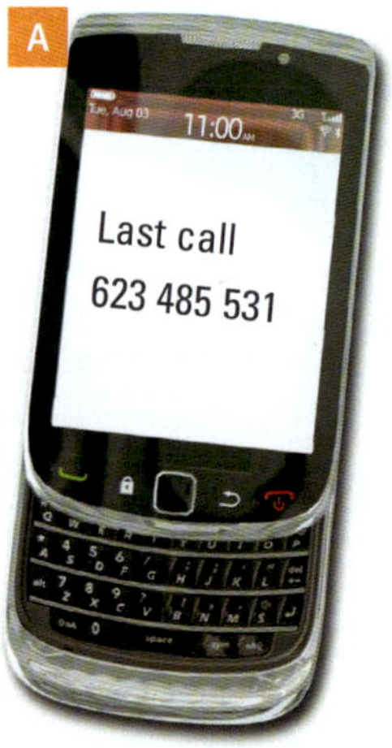

B
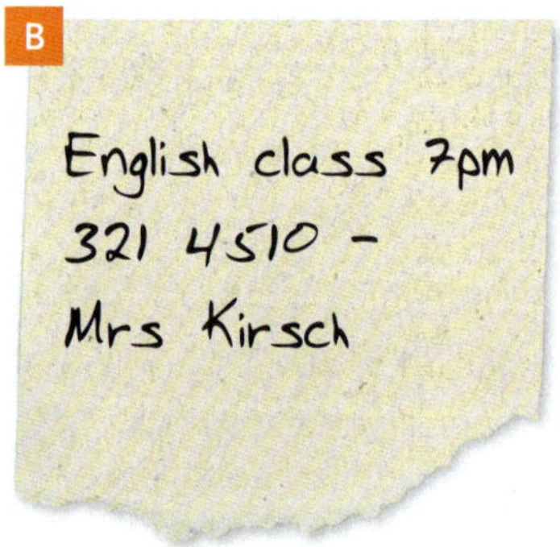

C

D

2 1.14 Listen again and say the numbers in the pictures in exercise 1.

FUNCTIONAL LANGUAGE: asking for & saying phone numbers

1 1.15 Read and listen.

A: What's your phone number?
B: It's 928 2914.
A: My phone number is 926 0438.

Language note

Say *zero* or *oh* for phone numbers in English.

2 1.16 Listen and repeat the phone numbers.

1 687 054 265
2 44 0378 543 0157
3 350 2871

3 What's your phone number? Tell a partner.

GRAMMAR: *it*

My phone number is 966 0438. ***It's*** *966 0438.*
It's – It ***is***
Use *it* for things.

SEE LANGUAGE REFERENCE PAGE 22

1 Replace the words in *italics* with *he* or *it*.

1 Where is Mark from?
Mark is from Britain.
2 Mary is from Glasgow.
Glasgow is in Scotland.
3 What's her phone number?
Her phone number is 753 891.

2 1.17 Listen to the recording to check your answers.

PRONUNCIATION: intonation (1)

1 1.18 Listen to the intonation in these questions.

How are you? Where are you from?
What's your name? What's your phone number?

2 1.18 Listen again and repeat the questions. Copy the intonation.

SPEAKING

1 1.19 Read and listen to the dialogue.

A: What's your mobile number?
B: It's 0793 812 9421.
A: OK. What's your home number?
B: It's 928 2914.
A: What's your work number?
B: Sorry, I don't have one.

2 Complete the chart with your phone numbers.

Phone numbers	You	Student 1	Student 2
Home			
Work			
Mobile			

3 Talk to two other students. Complete the chart with their phone numbers.

Useful language

What's your home / work / mobile number?
It's …
OK.
Sorry, I don't have one.

1D | Review

Functional language

1 Complete the words.

1

2

3

4

2 1.20 Listen to check your answers. Repeat the phrases.

Reading & vocabulary

1 Read the text about three teachers and complete the table.

Name:				
From:				
Work number:				

2 Complete the table in exercise 1 with information about your teacher. Ask questions.

What's your name?
Where are you from?
What's your work number?

3 Write a text similar to exercise 1 about your teacher.

This is …

Grammar

1 Look at Reading & vocabulary exercise 1 on page 12. Complete the sentences with the correct form of the verb.

1 My name ____ Will Goodfellow.
2 I ____ from Australia.
3 They ____ Sofia and Olga.
4 Sofia ____ from Italy and Olga ____ from Germany.
5 She ____ from Frankfurt.
6 We ____ your teachers.
7 It ____ nice to meet you.

2 Make sentences about the people in the picture above.

His name is …
He's from …
His phone number …

3 Complete the sentences so that they are true for you.

My name …
I'm from …
My phone number …

Speaking

1 Work in pairs. Choose one of the pictures. Prepare a dialogue. Use the expressions in the Useful language box to help you.

A

B

2 Practise your dialogue. Then present your dialogue to another pair in the class.

Useful language

Hello./Hi./Goodbye./Bye.	
How are you?	*Fine, thanks.*
What's your name?	*My name is … /I'm …*
This is …	
Nice to meet you.	*Nice to meet you, too.*
Where are you from?	*I'm from …*

Self-assessment (✓)

☐ I can greet other people.
☐ I can introduce myself and other people.
☐ I can count to ten.
☐ I can say my phone number.
☐ I can say where I am from.

2A | Hotel lobby

Vocabulary: The alphabet; Numbers 11–20; Abbreviations
Functional language: Spelling names
Listening: At the hotel

Listening

1 Look at the photos. What city is it? What country is it?

2 1.21 Listen and check.

3 Who is at the hotel?

a) Tom and Emily b) Tom and Katy c) John and Katy

Vocabulary & pronunciation: the alphabet

1 1.22 Listen and repeat the alphabet.

ABCD EFG HIJK LMNOP QRS TUV WXYZ

2 1.23 Listen and say the letters in groups.

/eɪ/	A H J K
/iː/	B C D E G P T V
/e/	F L M N S X Z
/aɪ/	I Y
/əʊ/	O
/uː/	Q U W
/ɑː/	R

3 1.24 Listen and tick (✓) the name you hear the person spells.

1	Tom __	Tim __
2	Jen __	Jim __
3	Mike __	Mack __
4	Mary __	Marie __
5	Stephen __	Steven __

4 Work in pairs, A and B.

A: Spell the names from exercise 3.
B: Point at the correct name.

5 1.25 Look at the forms. There is a mistake in each name. Listen and correct the mistake.

1

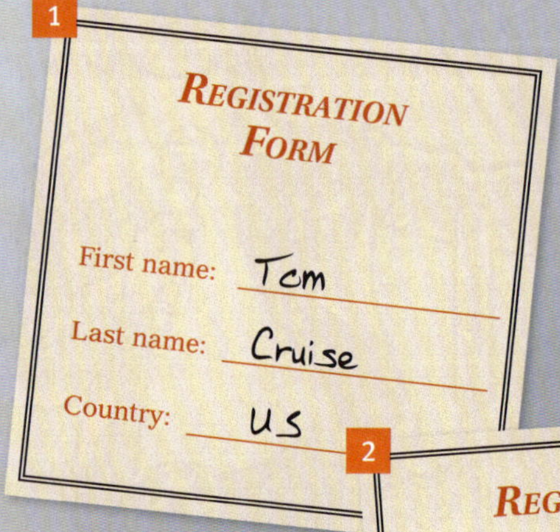
Registration Form

First name: Tom
Last name: Cruise
Country: US

2

Registration Form

First name: Kate
Last name: Middleton
Country: Britain

FUNCTIONAL LANGUAGE: spelling names

1 1.26 Listen and repeat.

A: How do you spell your *last name*?
B: C-R-E-W-E-S.

2 Spell your first name and last name.

3 Work in pairs, A and B.

A: Choose one of the British (first) names from *English around you* on page 7.
B: Ask A how to spell the name.

Swap roles and continue.

VOCABULARY & LISTENING: numbers 11–20

1 1.27 Listen and repeat the numbers.

2 1.28 Listen and complete with numbers.

Hotel Reservations

File Edit View Insert Format Help

Name	Room number
Tom Crewes	
Kate Middledown	
Mr and Mrs Bickham	
George Clunie	

SPEAKING

1 1.29 Read and listen to the dialogue.

Sarah: Excuse me. I have a reservation.
Receptionist: Yes, what's your name, please?
Sarah: Sarah Paline.
Receptionist: How do you spell your last name?
Sarah: P-A-L-I-N-E.
Receptionist: Thank you, Ms Paline. You're in room 15B.
Sarah: Thank you.

2 Work in pairs. Prepare a similar dialogue.

> *Useful language*
>
> *Excuse me.*
> *Please.*
> *Thank you.*

ENGLISH AROUND YOU: abbreviations

1 Read the abbreviations. How do you say them in English? What do they mean?

BBC IBM CNN
UK US FBI

2 1.30 Listen and check. Read audioscript 1.30 on page 120.

3 Do you know any other English abbreviations?

2B | Hotel room

Grammar: *This/that/here/there*
Vocabulary: Common objects
Reading & listening: Dialogue: in a hotel room

VOCABULARY: common objects

1 1.31 Look at the picture and listen to the words.

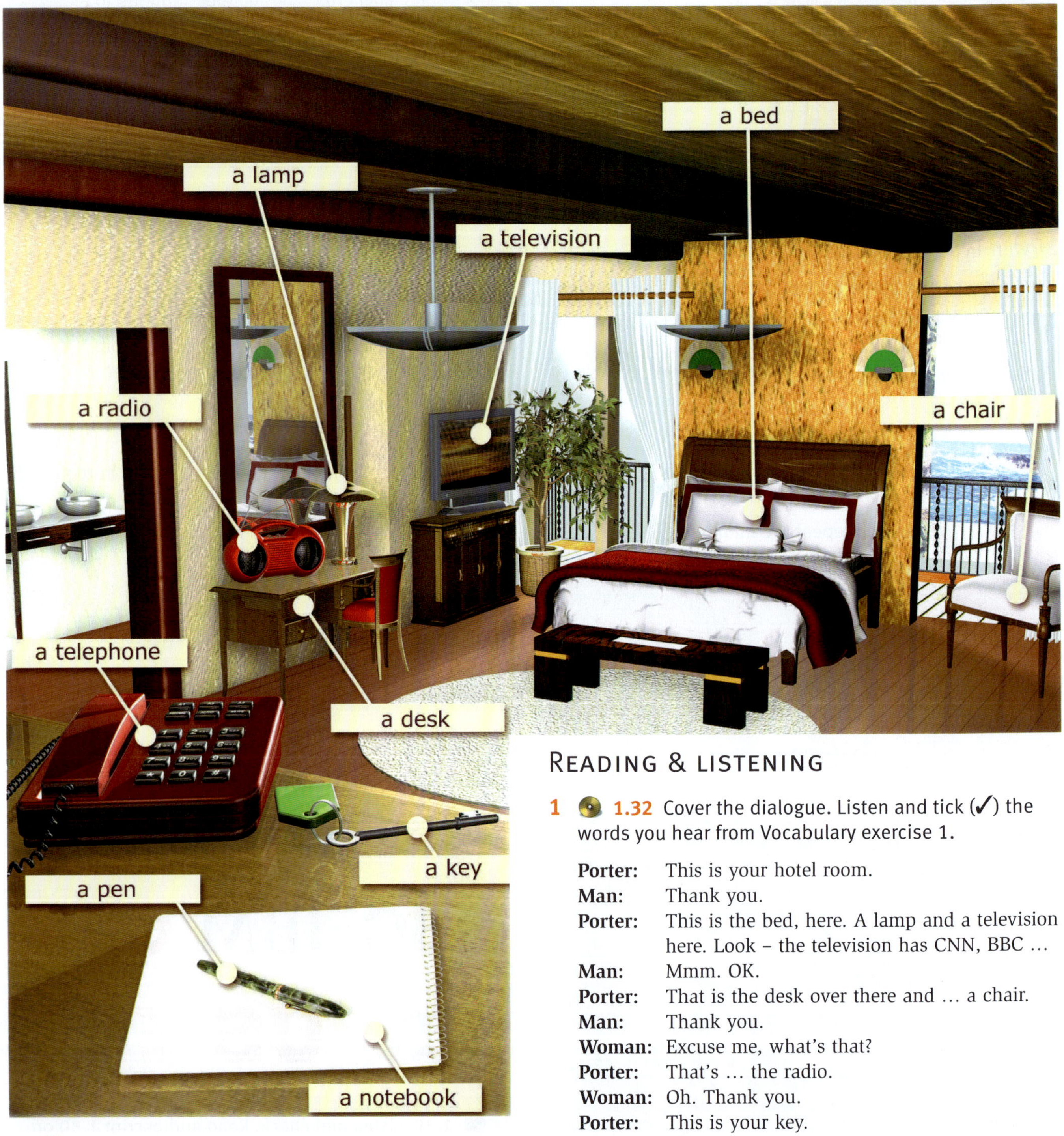

2 1.31 Listen again and repeat.

READING & LISTENING

1 1.32 Cover the dialogue. Listen and tick (✓) the words you hear from Vocabulary exercise 1.

Porter: This is your hotel room.
Man: Thank you.
Porter: This is the bed, here. A lamp and a television here. Look – the television has CNN, BBC …
Man: Mmm. OK.
Porter: That is the desk over there and … a chair.
Man: Thank you.
Woman: Excuse me, what's that?
Porter: That's … the radio.
Woman: Oh. Thank you.
Porter: This is your key.
Man: Thank you. Here you are.
Porter: Thank you!

2 1.32 Listen again. Read the dialogue and check your answers.

GRAMMAR: *this/that/here/there*

Here
What's ***this****?*
This *is a* + noun
There
What's ***that****?*
That *is a* + noun

The plural of *this* is *these*. The plural of *that* is *those*. Use *these* and *those* with plural nouns.

SEE LANGUAGE REFERENCE PAGE 22

1 Underline the correct word to complete the dialogues.

1
A: What's *this / that* in English?
B: It's a CD player.

2
A: What's *that / this*?
B: It's my phone.

3
A: Where is he?
B: He's *here / there*. In the hotel!

4
A: Is *this / that* your pen?
B: Yes, it is. Thank you.

5
A: Look over *there / here*!
B: Where?
A: It's Superman!

2 1.33 Listen and check your answers. Say the sentences with a partner.

SPEAKING

1 Work in small groups. One student points to an object on the page or in the class. Ask, *What's this/that in English?* Another student answers.

Useful language

What's this/that in English?
It's a …
I don't know.

2c Hotel café

Grammar: Plurals, *a/an*
Vocabulary: Food & drink
Listening: In a cafe

A

VOCABULARY: food & drink

1 Match the words in the box to the photos A–H.

> a coffee   a tea   a cheese sandwich
> a croissant   an orange juice   an omelette
> an apple juice   a mineral water

2 1.34 Listen and check.

3 1.34 Listen again and repeat the words.

B

C

D

E

F

G

H

Listening

1 1.35 Listen to some people at a café. Tick (✓) the food and drink on the menu you hear.

HOTEL PALACE CAFÉ

DRINKS

Coffee
Tea
Juice
Mineral water

FOOD

Cheese sandwich
Tuna sandwich
Croissant

TODAY'S SPECIAL:
Cheese and tomato omelette and a coffee 2€!

Grammar: plurals, *a/an*

Use *a/an* with singular nouns.
a + consonant
 a *sandwich*
an + vowel
 an *omelette*
To make nouns plural, add *-s* or *-es*.
 two coffees
 two sandwiches

See Language Reference page 22

1 Complete the phrases with *a* or *an*.

1 ___ orange juice
2 ___ sandwich
3 ___ key
4 ___ chair
5 ___ croissant
6 ___ apple juice
7 ___ bed
8 ___ desk

2 Choose the correct phrase or sentence, a or b.

1
a) Three coffee.
b) Three coffees.

2
a) A tuna sandwich, please.
b) An tuna sandwich, please.

3
a) I have two notebooks.
b) I have two notebook.

4
a) The omelette is two euro.
b) The omelette is two euros.

Pronunciation: /iː/

1 1.36 Listen to the underlined sound in these words.

cheese three please coffee speak

2 1.37 Listen and repeat the sentences.

1 Three teas and three coffees.
2 These are your keys.
3 Excuse me, please.

Functional language: in a café

1 1.38 Listen and repeat the dialogue.

A: I'd like a sandwich, please.
B: Would you like cheese or tuna?
A: Cheese, please.
B: Here you are.

2 Work in pairs. Turn to page 119.

3 Work in pairs, A and B.

A: You work in the café.
B: You are the customer.

Prepare a dialogue.

Use the Functional language and the menu in Listening exercise 1 to help you.

2D | Review

Functional language

1 Put the dialogue in the correct order.

☐ Gomez.
☐ *1* Hello.
☐ Thank you.
☐ Hello. What's your last name?
☐ G-O-M-E-Z.
☐ How do you spell your name?

2 1.39 Listen and check your answer.

3 Work in pairs. Make a similar dialogue.

Listening

1 1.40 Listen to four dialogues. Underline the correct spelling of British place names.

1 *Canbridge / Cambridge*
2 *Torquay / Torquee*
3 *Cheshere / Cheshire*
4 *Greenwich / Grennich*

2 Work in pairs. We have some strange place names in Britain – see one below. Do you know any strange place names? How do you spell them? Tell a partner.

Vocabulary

1 Match the words in the box to the objects A–I in the picture. There are three extra words you don't need.

a key a bed a chair a desk a pen
a television a notebook a telephone
a lamp a coffee a croissant an orange juice

2 Work in pairs. Cover the words. Test each other.

A: What's this in English?
B: It's a telephone.

3 Complete hotel key cards 1 and 2 with the name of a hotel and a room number.

4 Work in pairs. Ask and answer to find the information about the key cards from your partner. Write the information in key cards 3 and 4.

A: What is the name of your hotel?
B: It's …
A: What's your room number?
B: It's …

Grammar

1 Underline the correct word to complete the dialogues.

1

A: Hello.
B: Hello, I'd like two tuna *sandwiches / sandwich,* please.
A: Two *sandwiches / sandwich*.
B: Yes, and *an / a* orange juice, too, please.
A: Here you are. *One / Three* pounds, please.
B: Thank you.

2

A: Hi, I'm Martin.
B: Hello, Martin. This is your *desk / desks*.
A: Good.
B: This is your chair. Your phone is here, and *a / an* lamp … here.
A: Thank you. My key?
B: Oh, yes. Here you are. Two *keys / keyes* for you.
A: Thank you.

Self-assessment (✓)

- ☐ I can spell words.
- ☐ I can count to 20.
- ☐ I can ask what words are in English.
- ☐ I can ask for a drink or food in a café.

Grammar

To be: present simple

full form		contraction	
I am	from the US.	I'm	from the US.
You are		You're	
He is		He's	
She is		She's	
It is		It's	
We are		We're	
They are		They're	

It

Use *it* for things.

What's your phone number?
It*'s 9328 2289.*

Other contractions

What is your name? → *What****'s*** *your name?*
That is the hotel. → *That****'s*** *the hotel.*

My, his, her

My name is Adrian.

His name is Jack.

Her name is Paula.

This, that, here, there

Here

What's this?
This is a table.

There

What's that?
That is a chair.

Plurals, *a/an*

Use *a*, *an* with singular nouns.

a + consonant

a *sandwich,* ***a*** *table,* ***a*** *chair,* ***a*** *country*

an + vowel

an *omelette,* ***an*** *apple juice*

To make nouns plural, add *-s* or *-es*.

*Two coffee****s****, three sandwich****es****, phone****s****, key****s***

These, those

The plural of *this* is *these*.

This *pen.* ***These*** *pens.*

The plural of *that* is *those*.

That *key.* ***Those*** *keys.*

Functional language

Greetings

Hello./Hi.
Goodbye./Bye.
How are you?
I'm fine, thanks. And you?

Asking & saying names

What's your name?
My name's (Jack). What's your name?
I'm (Tania).

Meeting people

This is (Philip).
Nice to meet you.
Nice to meet you, too.

Asking & saying where you are from

Where are you from?
I'm from (Germany).

Asking & saying phone numbers

What's your phone number?
It's (928 2914).
My phone number is (932 82289).

In a café

I'd like a sandwich, please.
Would you like cheese or tuna?
Cheese, please.
Here you are.

Spelling names

How do you spell your first/last name?

Word list

Cities & countries

Australia *n*	/ɒˈstreɪliə/
Beijing *n*	/ˌbeɪˈdʒɪŋ, ˌbeɪˈʒɪŋ/
Brazil *n*	/brəˈzɪl/
Britain *n*	/ˈbrɪt(ə)n/
China *n*	/ˈtʃaɪnə/
France *n*	/frɑːns/
Frankfurt *n*	/ˈfræŋkfɜːt/
Germany *n*	/ˈdʒɜːməni/
Italy *n*	/ˈɪtəli/
London *n*	/ˈlʌndən/
Moscow *n*	/ˈmɒskəʊ/
New York *n*	/ˌnjuː ˈjɔː(r)k/
Paris *n*	/ˈpærɪs/
Rio de Janeiro *n*	/ˌriːəʊ də dʒəˈnɪərəʊ, ʒəˈnɪərəʊ/
Rome *n*	/rəʊm/
Russia *n*	/ˈrʌʃə/
Thailand *n*	/ˈtaɪlænd, ˈtaɪlənd/
the US *n*	/ðə ˌjuː ˈes/

Numbers 1–20

one ***	/wʌn/
two ***	/tuː/
three	/θriː/
four	/fɔː(r)/
five	/faɪv/
six	/sɪks/
seven	/ˈsev(ə)n/
eight	/eɪt/
nine	/naɪn/
ten	/ten/
eleven	/ɪˈlev(ə)n/
twelve	/twelv/
thirteen	/ˌθɜː(r)ˈtiːn/
fourteen	/ˌfɔː(r)ˈtiːn/
fifteen	/ˌfɪfˈtiːn/
sixteen	/ˌsɪksˈtiːn/
seventeen	/ˌsev(ə)nˈtiːn/
eighteen	/ˌeɪˈtiːn/
nineteen	/ˌnaɪnˈtiːn/
twenty	/ˈtwenti/

Common objects

bed *n* ***	/bed/
card *n* ***	/kɑː(r)d/
chair *n* ***	/tʃeə(r)/
desk *n* ***	/desk/
key *n* ***	/kiː/
lamp *n* **	/læmp/
mobile phone *n* **	/ˌməʊbaɪl ˈfəʊn/
notebook *n* *	/ˈnəʊtˌbʊk/
pen *n* **	/pen/
phone number *n* *	/ˈfəʊn ˌnʌmbə(r)/
radio *n* ***	/ˈreɪdiəʊ/
telephone *n* ***	/ˈtelɪfəʊn/
television *n* ***	/ˈtelɪˌvɪʒ(ə)n/

Food & drink

apple juice *n*	/ˈæp(ə)l ˌdʒuːs/
cheese *n* **	/tʃiːz/
sandwich *n* **	/ˈsæn(d)wɪtʃ/
coffee *n* ***	/ˈkɒfi/
croissant *n*	/ˈkwæsɒ̃/
mineral water *n*	/ˈmɪn(ə)rəl ˌwɔːtə(r)/
omelette *n*	/ˈɒmlət/
orange juice *n*	/ˈɒrɪndʒ ˌdʒuːs/
tea *n* ***	/tiː/

Other words & phrases

ask *v* ***	/ɑːsk/
café *n* **	/ˈkæfeɪ/
excuse me	/ɪkˈskjuːs ˌmi/
greeting *n* *	/ˈgriːtɪŋ/
home *n* ***	/həʊm/
hotel *n* ***	/həʊˈtel/
please ***	/pliːz/
popular *adj* ***	/ˈpɒpjʊlə(r)/
room *n* ***	/ruːm/
spell *v* **	/spel/
strange *adj* ***	/streɪndʒ/
thank you ***	/ˈθæŋk ˌjʊ/

3A International workers

Grammar: *To be* (affirmative)
Vocabulary: Jobs
Reading: *International workers*

READING

1 Read the texts. Match the people 1–5 to the photos A–E.

International workers

1 This is Sylvie. She's from France. She's a doctor.

2 He's Edward and she's Francesca. They're from Britain. They're police officers.

3 My name's Frank. I'm from the Czech Republic. I'm an aid worker.

4 This is James. He's from the US. He's a diplomat.

5 I'm Giovanni and this is Sabina. We're from Italy. We're architects.

____

____

____

____

2 Read the texts again and complete the table.

Name	Country	Job

VOCABULARY: jobs

1 1.41 Listen and repeat the jobs in the table in Reading exercise 2.

> *Language note*
>
> Use *a/an* with jobs.

2 Complete the sentences with *a* or *an*. What are these jobs in your language?

1 He's ____ teacher.
2 She's ____ doctor.
3 She's ____ student.
4 He's ____ actor.

3 1.42 Listen and repeat.

PRONUNCIATION: /dʒ/, /d/, /r/ & /tʃ/

1 1.43 Listen and repeat the sounds and words.

/dʒ/ job
/d/ doctor
/r/ radio
/tʃ/ teacher

2 1.44 Listen and repeat the sentences.

1 The job is in Germany.
2 My teacher is from China.
3 David is a doctor from Denmark.
4 Ruslan is a taxi driver from Russia.

FUNCTIONAL LANGUAGE: asking about jobs

1 1.45 Read and listen. Say the phrases.

What's your job?
What do you do?
I'm a teacher.

2 Talk to five people in the class. Ask about their jobs.

GRAMMAR: *to be* (affirmative)

*I **am*** *You **are*** *He/She/It **is***	*a student.*	*I'**m*** *You'**re*** *He'**s**/She'**s**/It'**s***	*a student.*
*We **are*** *They **are***	*students.*	*We'**re*** *They'**re***	*students.*

SEE LANGUAGE REFERENCE PAGE 40

1 Complete the sentences with *am*, *is* or *are*.

1 I ____ from Hong Kong.
2 My name ____ Yan Chee.
3 This ____ Mark.
4 He ____ a diplomat.
5 They ____ from Brazil.
6 You ____ a student.
7 We ____ architects.

2 Make the sentences with contractions.

1 I am a student.
I'm a student.
2 We are from Spain.
3 He is an executive.
4 They are doctors.
5 She is from Chicago.
6 You are an actor.

SPEAKING

1 Work in pairs, A and B.

A: Turn to page 114.
B: Turn to page 118.

Complete the job files.

> *Useful language*
>
> *His/Her name(s) is …*
> *Their phone number(s) is/are …*
>
> *He/She is from …/an actor.*
> *They are from …/actors.*
> *How do you spell that?*

3B International train

Grammar: *To be* (negative)
Vocabulary: Colours & nationalities
Listening: Dialogue on a train

VOCABULARY: colours & nationalities

1 1.46 Listen and repeat the colours.

red white blue black yellow green brown

2 1.47 Match the photos of international trains A–F to the phrases 1–6. Listen to check your answers.

1 a French train
2 an Italian train
3 a Polish train
4 a Chinese train
5 a German train
6 an American train

3 1.47 Listen again and repeat.

4 Describe the flags of the different countries.

The German flag is black, red and yellow.

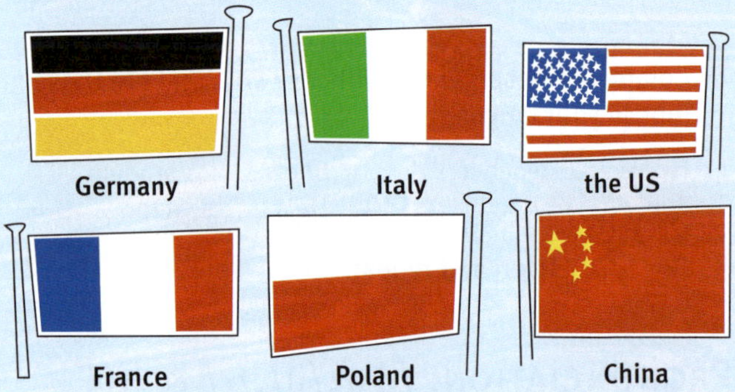

5 What's your nationality? What colour is the flag of your country?

I'm Canadian. The Canadian flag is red and white.

LISTENING

1 1.48 Listen to the dialogue. What is the problem?

2 1.48 Listen again and decide if the sentences are true (T) or false (F). Correct the false sentences.

1 They are on a train.
2 The woman is from France.
3 The man is from the US.
4 The train is the Spanish Express to Madrid.
5 The next stop is Milan.

GRAMMAR: *to be* (negative)

To make the negative of *to be*, add *not* or *n't* to the verb.

I'm ***not***
You aren't
He/She/It isn't on the train.
We aren't
They aren't

SEE LANGUAGE REFERENCE PAGE 40

1 1.49 Listen and correct the sentences.

1 Her name is Michelle. (Dominique)
Her name isn't Michelle. Her name is Dominique.
2 She is from France. (Switzerland)
3 His name is Brad. (Mike)
4 He's Canadian. (American)
5 They're on a plane. (train)
6 It's the Spanish Express. (Italian Express)

2 Complete the dialogues with the correct form of the verb *to be*.

1
A: This Italian coffee (1) ____ (+) good.
B: It (2) ____ (–) Italian coffee.
A: Excuse me?
B: It (3) ____ (–) Italian. It (4) ____ (+) Brazilian.
A: Really? Oh, yes, you (5) ____ (+) right. Brazilian coffee. Very good.

2
A: Where (6) ____ (+) you from in the United States?
B: We (7) ____ (–) American.
A: You (8) ____ (–) American?
B: No, we (9) ____ (+) from Canada.

3 1.50 Listen to the recording to check your answers. Practise the dialogues.

PRONUNCIATION: contractions (2)

1 1.51 Listen and tick (✓) the sentence you hear, a or b.

1
a) He is Scottish. __
b) He's Scottish. __

2
a) You are not David. __
b) You're not David. __

3
a) We are not Canadian. __
b) We're not Canadian. __

4
a) They are from France. __
b) They're from France. __

5
a) I am a student. __
b) I'm a student. __

6
a) I am not a teacher. __
b) I'm not a teacher. __

2 1.51 Listen again. Repeat the sentences.

SPEAKING

1 Read the sentences about famous people, things and places. Which sentence is correct?

1 Volkswagen is from Germany.
2 Tokyo is in China.
3 Barack Obama is from Brazil.

2 Correct the incorrect sentences in exercise 1.

Barack Obama isn't from Brazil. He's from the US.

3 Make three similar sentences about people, places or things: two incorrect and one correct.

4 Work in pairs, A and B.

A: Say your sentence.
B: Say, *Correct!* or correct the incorrect sentence.

3c International school

Grammar: *To be* (questions & short answers)
Vocabulary: Days of the week; The classroom
Reading: *United Nations International School*

Reading

1 Look at the photos and answer the questions.

1 What is UNIS?
2 Where is UNIS?

2 Read the text and check your answers.

File Edit View Favourites Tools Help Links

United Nations International School (UNIS)

UNIS is the United Nations International School. It's in New York. At the United Nations International School there are teachers from 70 different countries and students from 120 different countries. UNIS is open six days a week, from Monday to Saturday.

Vocabulary: days of the week

1 Complete the days of the week with a CAPITAL letter.

T T F S W M S

_onday _uesday
_ednesday _hursday
_riday _aturday
_unday

2 1.52 Listen to the recording to check your answers. Repeat the days of the week.

Listening

1 1.53 Listen to a teacher from UNIS answer questions about the school. Put the questions in the correct order.

☐ Where are the teachers from?
☐ When is the school open?
☐ Is the school cafeteria open every day?
☐ Who is the Director?
☐ Are you the Director?

2 1.53 Listen again and match the answers a–f to the questions 1–5 in exercise 1.

a Many teachers at UNIS are from the United States, but we also have French, German, Swiss, Italian, Japanese and Australian teachers.
b No, it isn't. The cafeteria isn't open on Saturdays.
c No, I'm not. I'm the Assistant Director.
d The Director is Mr Stuart Walker. He's in his office right now.
e The school is open Monday to Saturday.

GRAMMAR: *To be* (questions & short answers)

For *yes/no* questions, the subject and the verb change places.

The school ***is*** *open.*

Is *the school open?*

Short answers

Are *you English?*

Yes, *I* ***am.***/***No,*** *I'****m*** *not.*

For *wh-* questions, put the question words: *what, when, who* and *where* in front of the verb.

Where *are you from?*

When *is the school open?*

SEE LANGUAGE REFERENCE PAGE 40

1 Complete the questions with the correct form of the verb *to be*.

1 What ____ your name?
2 Where ____ you from?
3 ____ you Spanish?
4 ____ it Monday today?
5 ____ your teacher British?

2 1.54 Listen to the recording to check your answers. Answer the questions.

3 Make questions from the prompts.

1 Where / the school?
2 / the school / open on Saturday?
3 When / the school /open?
4 Where / the teachers / from?
5 Who / the Head of School?
6 / the Head of School / from Vietnam?
7 Where / the Head of School / from?

4 Work in pairs. Look at the information about UNIS Hanoi. Ask and answer the questions in exercise 3.

UNIS Hanoi

United Nations International School in Hanoi, Vietnam

Open:	Monday to Friday
Teachers from:	Vietnam, United States, France, New Zealand, Australia, Spain, Canada, Finland
Director:	Chip Barder, US

FUNCTIONAL LANGUAGE: saying goodbye

1 1.55 Read and listen.

See you!
See you later.
See you on Monday.
See you on Tuesday.

2 Practise with other students.

ENGLISH AROUND YOU: the classroom

1 1.56 Read and listen to the phrases. Tick (✓) the ones you understand.

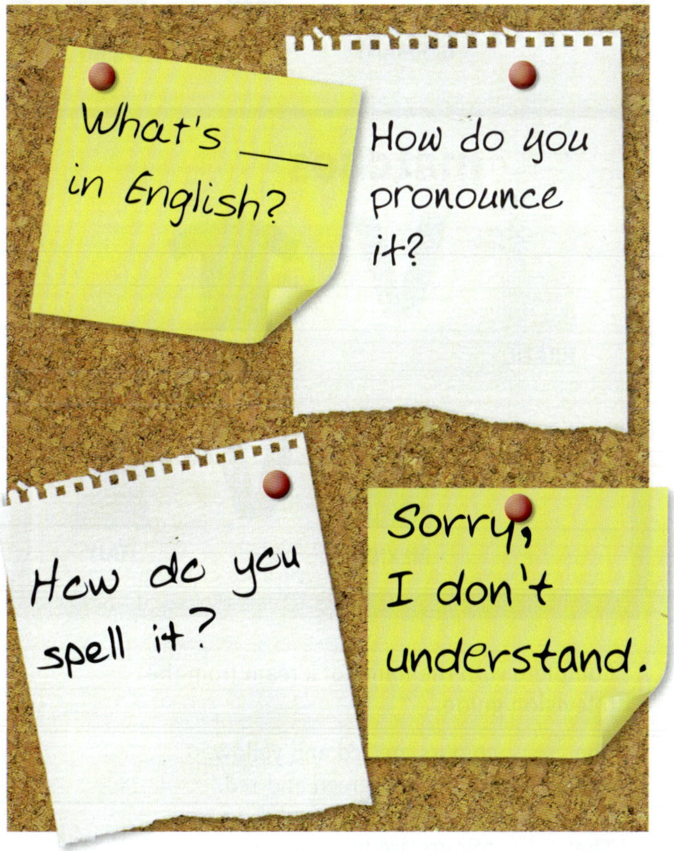

2 Work in pairs. Translate the phrases into your language.

3 What other English words or phrases are there in the classroom?

3D | Review

Reading & vocabulary

1 1.57 Read and listen to the television guide. When are the World Football matches? Complete with the correct day of the week.

2 Complete with the name of a team from the television guide.

1 The _____ colours are red and yellow.
2 The _____ colours are green and red.
3 The _____ colours are blue and red.
4 The _____ colours are blue and white.
5 The _____ colour is blue.
6 The _____ and _____ colour is white.
7 The _____ colour is yellow.

Grammar & vocabulary

1 Complete the sentences with the correct form of the verb *to be* and words from the box.

a teacher	actors	doctors
a taxi driver	a student	

1 They _____ _____.

2 She _____ _____.

3 They _____ _____.

4 She _____ _____.

5 He _____ _____.

2 1.58 Listen and check your answers. Say the sentences. Use contractions.

3 Cover the sentences in exercise 1. Work in pairs, A and B.

A: Say a sentence.
B: Point to the picture.

4 Swap roles and repeat.

Grammar

1 Match the questions 1–5 to the answers a–e.

1 Are you Italian?
2 Is he the teacher?
3 Are the students there?
4 Is she a doctor?
5 Is it Monday today?

a Yes, it is.
b Yes, they are.
c No, I'm not. I'm from Spain.
d No, she isn't. She's an ambulance driver.
e Yes, he is.

Speaking

1 Work in groups of three or four. Play *The International Student Game!*. Your teacher will explain the rules.

Self-assessment (✓)

- ☐ I can say my job.
- ☐ I can say where I'm from.
- ☐ I can ask about jobs.

The International Student Game!

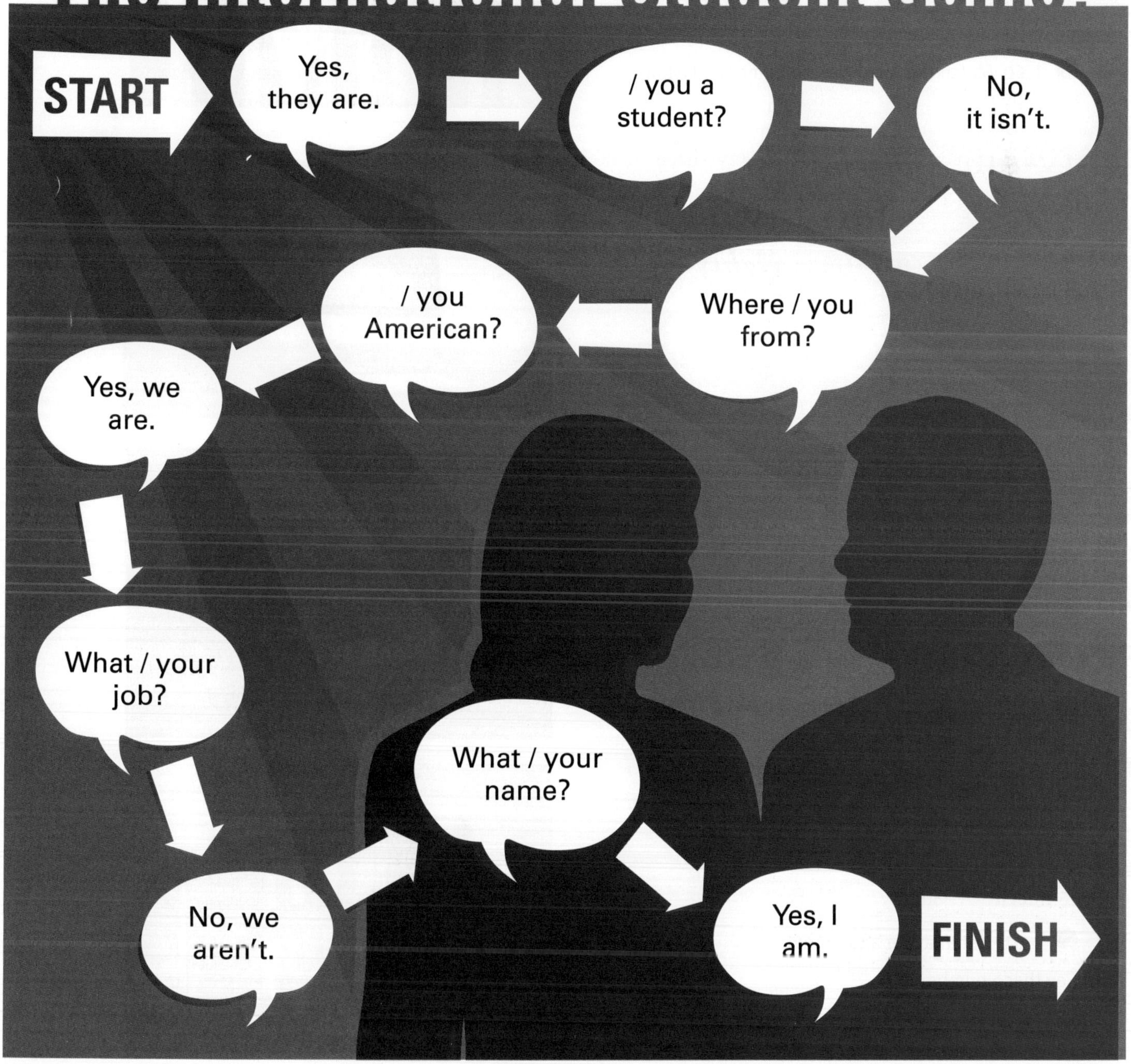

4A | Personal photos

Grammar: *It, they*
Vocabulary: Numbers 21–101
Listening: Dialogues about age

VOCABULARY: numbers 21–101

1 1.59 Listen and repeat.

20 twenty · 30 *thirty* · 70 *seventy* · 40 forty · 60 sixty · 80 eighty · 50 *fifty* · 90 ninety · 100 *one hundred (a hundred)*

2 1.60 Match the words to the numbers. Listen and repeat.

twenty-one · *fifty-six* · sixty-three · *thirty-five* · forty-two · ninety-nine · *seventy* · *eighty-eight* · one hundred and one

21 · 56 · 70 · 99 · 42 · 35 · 63 · 101 · 88

3 Work in pairs. Say three numbers to your partner. Your partner writes them down.

PRONUNCIATION: word stress (1)

1 1.61 Listen to the difference between these numbers.

☐ 13 thir**teen** ☐ 30 **thir**ty
☐ 14 four**teen** ☐ 40 **for**ty
☐ 15 fif**teen** ☐ 50 **fif**ty

2 1.61 Listen again and repeat.

3 Say these numbers.

16 60 17 70
18 80 19 90

LISTENING

1 1.62 Listen and match the speakers 1–4 to the photos A–D.

A

B

C

D

2 1.62 Listen again and complete the sentences.

1 The car is _____ years old.
2 The babies are _____ months old.
3 The house is _____ years old.
4 The computer is _____ months old.

Language note

There are *24 hours in a day.*
seven days in a week.
four weeks in a month.
twelve months in a year.

3 Work in pairs and answer the question.

- Do you have personal photos with you? If yes, describe them to your partner.

FUNCTIONAL LANGUAGE: talking about age

1 1.63 Read and listen.

How old is it?
It's five years old.
How old are you?
I'm thirty (years old).

2 1.63 Listen again and repeat.

3 Look at the difference.

1 He's an old man. He's a young man.

2 It's an old computer. It's a new computer.

4 1.64 Listen and repeat the sentences.

GRAMMAR: *it, they*

Use *it* for things.
The house is 70 years old.
***It**'s 70 years old.*
Use *they* for people or things.
The computers are two years old.
***They**'re two years old.*
The babies are thirteen months old.
***They**'re thirteen months old.*

SEE LANGUAGE REFERENCE PAGE 40

1 Read the sentences and replace the <u>underlined</u> word(s) with *he, she, it* or *they*.

1 The house is in Switzerland. <u>The house</u> is in Geneva. <u>The house</u> isn't new. <u>The house</u> is 120 years old.
2 These mobile phones are from Japan. <u>The mobile phones</u> are new. <u>The mobile phones</u> are only six months old.
3 This is Mark and Sylvia. <u>Mark and Sylvia</u> are French students. <u>Sylvia</u> is from England and <u>Mark</u> is from Scotland. This is their school. <u>Their school</u> is in Paris. <u>Their school</u> is fifteen years old.

2 1.65 Listen to the recording to check your answers. Read the texts out loud.

SPEAKING

1 Work in pairs. Ask each other questions with *How old ...?*

Useful language

Sorry, I don't have one.
I don't know.
I think he's 40 years old.
She's young/old.
It's new/old.

4B | Personal web page

Grammar: Possessive 's
Vocabulary: Family; Family words
Reading: Family album web page

Reading

1 Look at the family album web page. What are the people in the family called?

File Edit View Favourites Tools Help Links

www.personal-webpage.com/family/murphy.zr

PW PERSONAL WEB PAGE

Home | Photo Archive | Special Events | Updates | Message Boards | Email

Michael and Jennifer Murphy's family album

This is our new baby, Sean.
He's sixteen months old now!

My wife's parents: Donna and Martin.
They are from Oxford. They're teachers.

This is my grandparents' house in Cork, Ireland. The house is two hundred years old.

This is my sister, Sharon with her friend, Diane. Diane's American. She's an actor.

2 Read the web page again and answer the questions.

1 How old is Sean?
2 Where is the grandparents' house?
3 Where is Diane from?
4 What is Diane's job?
5 Where are Donna and Martin from?
6 What is their job?

3 Work in pairs. Discuss the question.

Do you or your family have a web page? If so, describe it to your partner.

Vocabulary: family

1 1.66 Listen and repeat the family words. What are they in your language?

1 a husband and wife
2 a father, mother, and their son and daughter
3 a mother and her children
4 grandparents, parents and children

2 Complete the table with the correct words from exercise 1.

wife		

3 Put these words in the correct column in exercise 2. What are they in your language?

grandmother grandfather brother sister

4 Work in pairs. Answer the questions.

1 Which of the families in exercise 1 is more common in your country?
2 How old are people in your country when they …
a) get married?
b) have children?
c) have grandchildren?

Pronunciation /ə/

1 1.67 Listen to how the underlined sound is pronounced in these words.

father mother daughter actor
umbrella doctor

2 1.68 Listen and repeat the sentences. Pronounce the underlined sounds as /ə/.

1 My father is an actor.
2 My mother is from America. She's American.
3 On Saturday, I'm with my grandparents.

Grammar: possessive 's

Use *'s* to show possession.
My wife's parents.

If the word ends in *s*, put the *'* after the *s*.
My grandparents' house.

See Language Reference page 40

1 Find all the examples of *'s* in the web page on page 34. Decide if they are possessive *'s* or contraction *'s*.

2 Complete the sentences about the Murphy family.

1 Donna is Jennifer's ____.
2 Michael is Jennifer's ____.
3 Michael is Sharon's ____.
4 Sean is Michael and Jennifer's ____.
5 Jennifer is Martin's ____.

3 Make other sentences about the Murphys. Use the possessive.

Sean → Michael
Sean is Michael's son.
1 Sean → Jennifer
2 Jennifer → Michael
3 Donna and Martin → Jennifer
4 Martin → Sean

Speaking

1 Write the names of three people from your family on a piece of paper.

2 Prepare a short presentation about these people. Use the phrases below for ideas of what to say.

This is …	*They are my …*
His name is …	*He's a …*
She's from …	*He's … years old.*

3 When you are ready, tell a partner about the people.

English around you: family words

1 1.69 Read and listen to these different informal family words. What do they mean?

kids gran grandad mum dad

4c | Personal possessions

Grammar: Prepositions of place
Vocabulary: Personal possessions
Listening: In a flat

VOCABULARY: personal possessions

1 1.70 Look at the pictures and listen to the words.

glasses

sunglasses

a jacket

a wallet

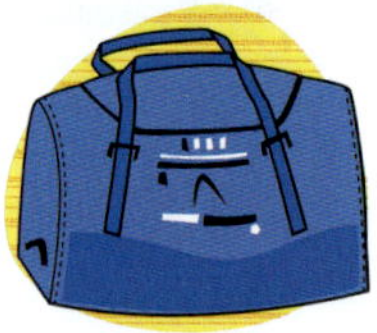
a bag

keys

an mp3 player

a mobile phone

a photo

an ID card

money

an umbrella

2 1.70 Listen again and repeat the words.

3 What is in your bag today? Tell a partner.

keys, photos, a wallet …

LISTENING

1 1.71 Mark and Lee are friends. Listen to three short dialogues. What does Lee want in each dialogue?

2 1.71 Listen again. Match the words in the box to the places A–C in the photo. There are two extra words.

glasses	bag	keys	wallet	money

Grammar: prepositions of place

In, on, under, next to, behind and *in front of* are prepositions of place.
Put them before the noun.

It's ***on*** *the table.*
Is it ***under*** *the table?*
It isn't ***in*** *my bag.*
It's ***next to*** *you.*

See Language Reference page 40

1 Where are Lee's things? Make sentences. Read audioscript 1.71 on page 122 to check your answers.

2 Rearrange the words to make sentences.

1 jacket the The on table is .
2 book glasses The are on the .
3 the table under are The keys .
4 The door the front in table is of .
5 sandwich The under the newspapers is .

3 Make sentences from the prompts. Use these words and a preposition of place.

1 The man / the table

2 The dog / the bath

Speaking

1 Work in pairs, A and B.

A: Turn to page 115.
B: Turn to page 117.

Describe and draw your pictures.

3 It / you!

4 The cat / the bed

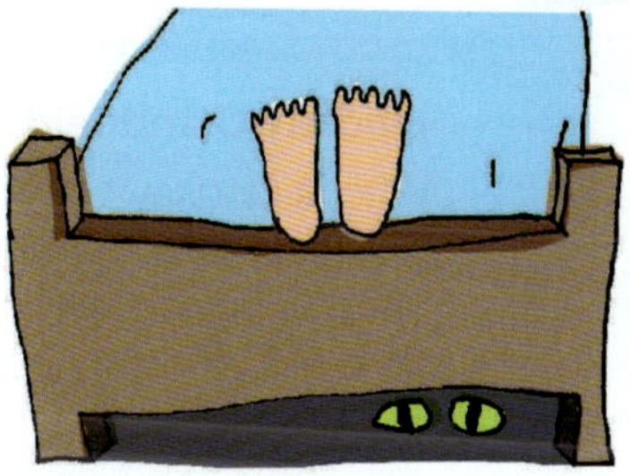

5 John / George

6 The woman / the boy

4D Review

Reading

File Edit View Favourites Tools Help Links

PERSONAL PROFILE Home Profile Find people Settings Help Sign out twitter

Lindsay Clandfield

@lclandfield Elche, usually

I write books for teachers and learners of English. I blog at a website, Six Things. I tweet on & off.

Lindsay Clandfield, Male, Married, 40 years old

Who is Lindsay? I'm an English teacher. I'm from Toronto, Canada. My family is from England. I'm the author of *Straightforward Beginner Second edition*. It's a book for English language students. Where is Lindsay now? In Spain.

1 Read the personal profile above. Complete the sentences with the correct words.

1 Lindsay is ____ years old.
2 He is an ____ ____.
3 He is from ____.
4 His family is from ____.
5 He is the author of ____.
6 It is a book for ____.
7 Lindsay Clandfield is in ____.

1.72 Listen to the recording to check your answers.

2 Make a similar personal profile for you.

Vocabulary

1 Make words from the cards.

sun	grand	let	ket
sev	wal	teen	parent
jac	fif	glasses	enty

2 Work in pairs, A and B.

A: Draw an object from page 36.
B: Guess the object.

3 Swap roles and repeat.

Functional language

1 Complete the sentences with a word or letters. The first one has been done for you.

1 How *old* is **it**?
It's ten years old.
2 How old are you?
She's twenty-nine and I'm twenty-four years ______.
3 Is he eighteen ______ old?
No, **he** isn't. He's sixteen.
4 How old are **they**?
They'______ seven weeks old.
5 How old is **she**?
She'______ ninety-five years old.

2 Think of a word or words to replace the words in **bold** in exercise 1.

A: How old is your car?
B: It's ten years old.

Grammar

This is my sister, Lisa. Lisa is a architect.
Lisa husband is a teacher. His name are James.
They Canadian. James is from Montreal and Lisa's is from Toronto.

1 Correct the five grammatical mistakes in the text.

2 Make a similar text about two people in your family.

This is …

Speaking

1 Work in pairs. Look at Lindsay's office. Ask and answer questions about the objects.

A: Where's the computer?
B: It's on the table.

Self-assessment (✓)

- ☐ I can count to 100.
- ☐ I can talk about age.
- ☐ I can talk about my family.
- ☐ I can say where things are in relation to other things.

Grammar

To be: present simple

affirmative				
full form			**contraction**	
I	am	from Canada.	I'm	fine.
He/She/It	is		He's/She's/It's	
You/We/They	are		You're/We're/They're	

To make the verb *to be* negative, add *not* (or *n't*) to the verb.

negative	
full form	**contraction**
I am not from Spain.	I'm not from Spain.
He/She/It is not a teacher.	He/She/It isn't a teacher.
You/We/They are not in class.	You/We/They aren't in class. or You're/We're/They're not in class.

To make questions with the verb *to be*, put the verb before the subject.

verb **subject**
Are *you married?*

question		
Am	I	30 years old?
Is	he/she/it	
Are	you/we/they	
short answer		
Yes, No,	I	am 'm not.
	he/she/it	is. isn't.
	you/we/they	are. aren't.

It, they

It and *they* are pronouns.

Use *it* for things.

*The house is in London. **It** is in London.*

Use *they* for people or things.

*The houses are in London. **They** are in London.*
*Philip and Katy are English. **They** are English.*

Possessive *'s*

Use *'s* to show possession.

*John**'s** mother.*
*My sister**'s** friend.*

If the word ends in an *-s*, add *'*.

His parents' house.
Not ~~*The house of his parents.*~~
The babies' rooms.
Not ~~*The room of the babies.*~~

Prepositions

in

on

under

next to

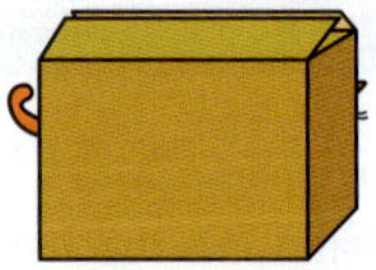

behind

in front of

FUNCTIONAL LANGUAGE

Asking about jobs

What's your job?
What do you do?
I'm a/an …

Saying goodbye

See you!
See you later.
See you on (Monday).

Talking about age

How is it?
It's five years old.

How old are you?
I'm thirty (years old).

WORD LIST

Jobs

actor *n* ***	/ˈæktə(r)/
aid worker *n*	/ˈeɪd ˌwɜː(r)ə(r)/
architect *n* **	/ˈɑː(r)kɪˌtekt/
author *n* ***	/ˈɔːθə(r)/
diplomat *n*	/ˈdɪpləmæt/
doctor *n* ***	/ˈdɒktə(r)/
driver *n* ***	/ˈdraɪvə(r)/
executive *n* **	/ɪɡˈzekjʊtɪv/
police officer *n* *	/pəˈliːs ˌɒfɪsə(r)/
student *n* ***	/ˈstjuːd(ə)nt/
teacher *n* ***	/ˈtiːtʃə/

Colours & nationalities

American *adj*	/əˈmerɪkən/
black *adj* ***	/blæk/
blue *adj* ***	/bluː/
Brazilian *adj*	/brəˈzɪliən/
brown *adj* ***	/braʊn/
Canadian *adj*	/kəˈneɪdiən/
Chinese *adj*	/ˌtʃaɪˈniːz/
French *adj*	/frentʃ/
German *adj*	/ˈdʒɜː(r)mən/
green *adj* ***	/ɡriːn/
Italian *adj*	/ɪˈtæljən/
Japanese *adj*	/ˌdʒæpəˈniːz/
Polish *adj*	/ˈpəʊlɪʃ/
red *adj* ***	/red/
Spanish *adj*	/ˈspænɪʃ/
white *adj* ***	/waɪt/
yellow *adj* ***	/ˈjeləʊ/

Days of the week

Saturday *n* ***	/ˈsætə(r)deɪ/
Sunday *n* ***	/ˈsʌndeɪ/
Monday *n* ***	/ˈmʌndeɪ/
Tuesday *n* ***	/ˈtjuːzdeɪ/
Wednesday *n* ***	/ˈwenzdeɪ/
Thursday *n* ***	/ˈθɜː(r)zdeɪ/
Friday *n* ***	/ˈfraɪdeɪ/

Numbers 21–101

twenty-one	/ˌtwenti ˈwʌn/
thirty-four	/ˌθɜː(r)ti ˈfɔː(r)/
forty-two	/ˌfɔː(r)ti ˈtuː/
fifty-six	/ˌfɪfti ˈsɪks/
sixty-three	/ˌsɪksti ˈθriː/
seventy-seven	/ˌsev(ə)nti ˈsev(ə)n/
eighty-eight	/ˌeɪti ˈeɪt/
ninety-nine	/ˌnaɪnti ˈnaɪn/
one hundred	/ˌwʌn ˈhʌndrəd/
one hundred and one	/wʌn ˌhʌndrəd ənd ˈwʌn/

Family

brother *n* ***	/ˈbrʌðə(r)/
child *n* ***	/tʃaɪld/
daughter *n* ***	/ˈdɔːtə(r)/
father *n* ***	/ˈfɑːðə(r)/
grandfather *n* **	/ˈɡræn(d)ˌfɑːðə(r)/
grandmother *n* **	/ˈɡræn(d)ˌmʌðə(r)/
grandparents *n* *	/ˈɡræn(d)ˌpeərənts/
husband *n* ***	/ˈhʌzbənd/
mother *n* ***	/ˈmʌðə(r)/
parents *n* ***	/ˈpeərənts/
sister *n* ***	/ˈsɪstə(r)/
son *n* ***	/sʌn/
wife *n* ***	/waɪf/

Personal possessions

bag *n* ***	/bæɡ/
glasses *n* *	/ˈɡlɑːsɪz/
ID card *n*	/ˌaɪ ˈdiː kɑː(r)d/
jacket *n* ***	/ˈdʒækɪt/
keys *n* ***	/kiːz/
mobile phone *n* **	/ˌməʊbaɪl, ˌməʊb(ə)l ˈfəʊn/
money *n* ***	/ˈmʌni/
mp3 player *n*	/em piː ˈθriː ˌpleɪə(r)/
photo *n* ***	/ˈfəʊtəʊ/
sunglasses *n*	/ˈsʌnˌɡlɑːsɪz/
umbrella *n* *	/ʌmˈbrelə/
wallet *n*	/ˈwɒlɪt/

Other words & phrases

ambulance *n* **	/ˈæmbjʊləns/
baby *n* ***	/ˈbeɪbi/
car *n* ***	/kɑː(r)/
correct *adj* ***	/kəˈrekt/
day *n* ***	/deɪ/
flag *n* **	/flæɡ/
hour *n* ***	/ˈaʊə(r)/
house *n* ***	/haʊs/
international *adj* ***	/ˌɪntə(r)ˈnæʃ(ə)nəl/
kid *n* ***	/kɪd/
new *adj* ***	/njuː/
old *adj* ***	/əʊld/
train *n* ***	/treɪn/
week *n* ***	/wiːk/
year *n* ***	/jɪə(r)/
young *adj* ***	/jʌŋ/

5A | Working life

Grammar: Present simple (1) (affirmative)
Vocabulary: Common verbs & nouns (1)
Reading: *Working life*

VOCABULARY: common verbs & nouns (1)

1 1.73 Look at the photo. Listen and repeat the sentences.

I live in Mexico City.
I work for a big company.
I go to work by taxi.

2 Complete the tables with words from the box.

a house   an office   car

I work	for	a big company.
	in	____. a factory. a shop.

I live	in	Mexico City. ____. a flat.
	with	my parents. my family. my wife and children.
	alone.	

I go	to school/to work	by	____. train. bus.
		on	foot.

3 Make three sentences about you. Use the phrases from exercise 2.

READING

1 Read the article on page 43. Match the paragraphs 1–3 to the photos A–C.

2 Read the article again. Who is speaking? Write *C* (Charri), *K* (Keith) or *TC* (Tom and Christine).

1 We're teachers. __
2 I work in a factory. __
3 I go to work by train. __
4 I live in London. __
5 We live next to Oaxaca. __
6 I go to work on foot. __

GRAMMAR: present simple (1) (affirmative)

Use the present simple to talk about things that are true.
They ***live*** *in Mexico.*
She ***works*** *in a factory.*
I ***go*** *to work by car.*

SEE LANGUAGE REFERENCE PAGE 58

1 Find all examples of the verbs *go*, *live* and *work* in the article. Complete the rule.

After *he*, *she* or *it*, add ____ to the verb in the present simple.

2 Choose the correct option, a or b.

1
a) I work in London. __
b) I works in London. __

2
a) They lives in Japan. __
b) They live in Japan. __

3
a) He works in a car factory. __
b) He work in a car factory. __

4
a) We live with our parents. __
b) We lives with our parents. __

5
a) Vanessa goes to school by bus. __
b) Vanessa go to school by bus. __

WORKING LIFE

1
Keith Wright lives in London. He's an actor and he works in a restaurant. He goes to work by train. Keith lives in a flat. He lives with two other actors.

2
Tom and Christine are American. They live in Mexico. They're teachers and they work at the University of Oaxaca. Their house is in a small town. The town is next to Oaxaca and they go to work by bus.

3
Charri is from the Philippines. She lives in Manila. She lives with her grandparents, her parents, her husband and children. She works in a factory. Every day, Charri goes to work on foot. The factory is two hours from her house.

3 Complete the text with verbs from the box in the correct form.

live (x2)   work (x2)   go

I (1) _____ with my brother, Josh. We (2) _____ in a house. The house is in the centre of San Francisco. I (3) _____ in an office. Josh is a shop assistant. He (4) _____ in a bookshop. The bookshop and the office are in the centre of San Francisco. We (5) _____ to work on foot.

SPEAKING

1 Prepare a short text about you. Use the article in Reading exercise 1 to help you.

2 Work in pairs. Tell your partner about you.

3 Work with a new student. Talk about your partner.

He/She lives in …
He/She lives with …
He/She works in …

5B | Technology life

Grammar: Present simple (2) (negative; *and* & *but*)
Vocabulary: Technology; Computers
Listening: Dialogues about technology

VOCABULARY: technology

1 Match the words 1–10 to the photos A–J.

1 a computer	6 a printer
2 an email address	7 a webcam
3 a website	8 a game console
4 an mp3 player	9 a digital camera
5 a mobile phone	10 a tablet computer

A

B

C
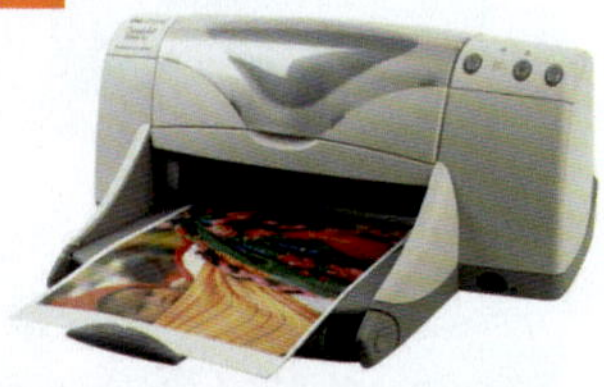

D
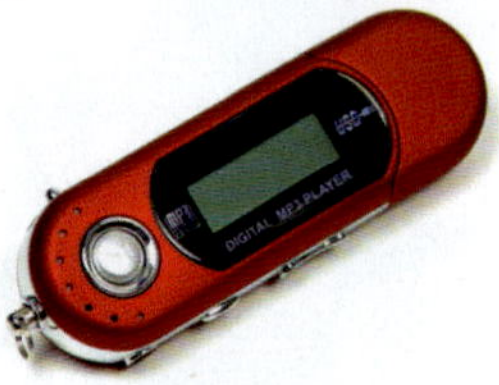

E

F

G

H

I

J

2 1.74 Listen and repeat the words.

3 Do you have these things at work, at school or at home? Tell a partner.

We have computers at work.
I have a digital camera at home.

> ***Language note:*** **have**
>
> The present simple of *have* has two forms, *have* and *has*.
> *I, you, we, they* ***have***
> *he, she, it* ***has***

FUNCTIONAL LANGUAGE: emails

1 1.75 Listen and repeat how we say these words and symbols in English.

@ at . dot / slash com com

2 1.76 Listen and repeat the dialogue.

A: What's your email address?
B: It's veronica@hotmail.sf.

3 What's your email address? Ask three people in the class.

A: What's your email address?
B: It's .../Sorry, I don't have one.

LISTENING

1 1.77 Listen to people talking about technology and their work. Tick (✓) the words in the box you hear.

computer	mobile phone	website	email
office	digital camera	car	

2 1.77 Listen again and decide if the sentences are true (T) or false (F). Correct the false sentences.

Dialogue 1
1 The woman writes personal emails at work.
2 The man has a mobile phone.

Dialogue 2
3 The man's wife has one computer at work.
4 The man and woman don't have a computer at home.

Dialogue 3
5 The machine is a tablet computer.
6 The woman doesn't use the tablet computer.

GRAMMAR: present simple (2) (negative; *and* & *but*)

Use *don't/doesn't* to make the negative in the present simple.

*I **don't** have an email address.*
*She **doesn't** have a computer at home.*

Use *and* or *but* to link words or phrases.
And gives more information.

*I have a computer **and** I use it.*

But shows a contrast.

*We have a fax machine, **but** we don't use it.*

SEE LANGUAGE REFERENCE PAGE 58

1 Complete the sentences. Put the verb in brackets into the correct form.

1 I ____ (*not write*) personal emails.
2 I ____ (*not know*) anything about computers or technology.
3 We ____ (*use*) the computers a lot. We ____ (*have*) a fax machine, but we ____ (*not use*) it. Everything is email now.

2 Tick (✓) the sentences that are true for your teacher. Change the sentences that aren't true.

1 The teacher has a computer. __
2 He/She has an email address. __
3 He/She goes to work by bus. __
4 He/She lives next to the school. __
5 He/She has three brothers and sisters. __

3 Complete the sentences with *and* or *but*.

1 She lives in Spain ____ she works in Spain.
2 She lives in Spain ____ she works in France.
3 He has a computer at work ____ he has a computer at home.
4 He has a computer at work ____ he doesn't have a computer at home.

PRONUNCIATION: /s/ & /z/

1 1.78 Listen and repeat the sounds and words.

/s/	/z/
works	has
seven	Brazil
desk	please
Spain	does

2 1.79 Listen and repeat the sentences.

1 The student's name is Samantha.
2 She works in Spain.
3 She has two mobile phones.
4 She doesn't use computers.

SPEAKING

1 Read the *Technology Life Survey*. Tick (✓) or cross (✗) the boxes.

TECHNOLOGY LIFE SURVEY

AT HOME	have	use
a computer	☐	☐
a mobile phone	☐	☐
a digital camera	☐	☐
a tablet computer	☐	☐
an email address	☐	☐
AT WORK/SCHOOL		
a computer	☐	☐
an email address	☐	☐
AT WORK		
a mobile phone	☐	☐

2 Work in pairs. Tell your partner about technology and you.

I have a computer at home and at work.
I use a computer at work, but I don't use a computer at home.

ENGLISH AROUND YOU: computers

1 Many computer words are English. Tick (✓) the words you know. What are these words in your language?

screen   mouse   World Wide Web   print
delete   save   cancel   load

2 1.80 Listen and repeat the words in exercise 1.

3 What other computer words do you know in English?

5c | Hard life?

Grammar: Present simple (3) (questions & short answers)
Vocabulary: Adjectives (1)
Reading & listening: Interview with a man about his new job

Reading & listening

1 Look at the picture of Lord Duncan. What does he do?

2 1.81 Read and listen to the interviewer (I) who is interviewing Lord Duncan (Lord D) about his new job. Does he have a hard life?

I: Lord Duncan, nice to meet you. You are the new President of Duncan Enterprises. Tell us about your new job.
Lord D: It's an interesting job, but it isn't easy.
I: Really?
Lord D: Well, I have my father's job. I work a lot.
I: Do you work every day?
Lord D: No, I don't. Not every day. I work from Monday to Wednesday.
I: Do you work in your father's old office?
Lord D: No, I don't. I have my own offices now.
I: Offices? Do you have more than one office?
Lord D: Yes, I do. I have two offices. One for me and one for the two secretaries.
I: I see. Two secretaries. Do they work Monday to Wednesday?
Lord D: No, no, no. No, they don't. They work Monday to Saturday.
I: Ah.
Lord D: I have a game of golf today. Do you have any other questions?
I: No, I don't. Thank you, Lord Duncan.
Lord D: You're welcome.

3 Read the interview again and choose the correct answer, a, b or c.

1 Lord Duncan is the ____ of Duncan Enterprises.
a) secretary
b) student
c) President

2 He works ____ a week.
a) five days
b) two days
c) three days

3 Lord Duncan's father ____ in the company.
a) lives
b) doesn't work
c) works

4 Lord Duncan has ____
a) two offices and two secretaries.
b) two offices and a secretary.
c) an office and two secretaries.

Vocabulary: adjectives (1)

1 1.82 Listen and repeat the sentences.

It's a **difficult** job.
It's a **boring** job.
It's a **good** job.

2 Match the words in **bold** in exercise 1 to the opposites below.

1 bad
2 interesting
3 easy

3 Work in pairs. Make sentences about these jobs. Use the adjectives from exercises 1 and 2.

1 Lord Duncan's job
Lord Duncan has an easy job.
2 the President of your country
3 a teacher
4 a university student
5 a police officer

Language note

Adjectives can come in two places in a sentence.
- before a noun — *a **good** day*
- after the verb *to be* — *It's **good**.*

GRAMMAR: present simple (3) (questions & short answers)

To make questions in the present simple, use the auxiliary verb *do* + subject + infinitive.

***Do you work** every day?*

If the subject is *he/she/it*, use *does* + subject + infinitive.

***Does your father work** in the company?*

Short answers

Yes + subject + *do/does*
No + subject + *don't/doesn't*

Yes, I do.
No, he doesn't.

SEE LANGUAGE REFERENCE PAGE 58

1 Make questions and answers about Lord Duncan.

1 he / work on Monday? ✓
Does he work on Monday? Yes, he does.
2 he / go to work by bus? ✗
3 he / live next to the office? ✓
4 he / have two secretaries? ✓
5 he / work on Saturday? ✗
6 he / have an easy job? ✓

2 Rearrange the words to make questions.

1 to school go you Do bus by ?
2 in work an office you Do ?
3 a car you Do have ?
4 Saturday on work you Do ?

3 Work in pairs. Ask and answer the questions in exercise 2.

PRONUNCIATION: intonation (2)

1 1.83 Listen to the intonation in these questions.

Does he have a job?
Do you use a computer?
Are you a student?

2 1.83 Listen again and repeat the questions. Copy the intonation.

SPEAKING

1 Play *My new job – a hard life?* Work in pairs, A and B.

My new job – a hard life?

A: You have a new job. Choose one of the jobs in the photos. Don't tell B. Answer B's questions.
B: Ask questions about A's new job. Use the words below to help you. Guess A's new job.

DO YOU ...	
have	a difficult job? an easy job? a good job?
use	a computer?
work	with other people? alone? Monday to Friday?
work in	a hospital? a school? an office?
ARE YOU A/AN ...?	

2 Swap roles and repeat the activity.

5D | Review

READING

1 Work in two groups, A and B.

Group A: Read about Milo.
Group B: Read about Bertie.

It's a DOG'S LIFE

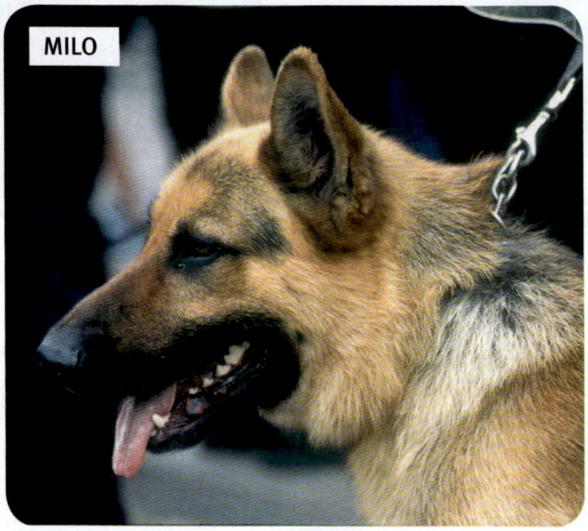

Milo is from America, but he lives in London. He goes to work Monday to Saturday. Milo works with the police. He is a police dog. He works in different places: at the airport, at schools and on the streets. Milo's partner is Officer Simon Pott. Simon and Milo work together and they live together. They're good friends.

Bertie is a British dog, but he doesn't live in Britain. He lives in Paris with his owner, Eugénie. Eugénie works for a French fashion magazine. Bertie doesn't work every day. He is a show dog and he goes to dog shows. The dog shows are in hotels in different cities: London, Madrid, Milan. When Bertie has a dog show, he and Eugénie go to the best hotel in town.

2 Answer the questions about the dog in your text.

1 Where is he from?
2 Where does he live?
3 Does he work every day?
4 Does he live alone?
5 Where does he work?
6 Does he have a difficult life?

3 Work with a partner from the other group. Compare your answers about the different dogs.

Grammar

1 Make questions from the prompts.

1 Milo / a police dog? *Is Milo a police dog?*
2 Milo / British?
3 Milo / work at the airport?
4 Simon and Milo / work together?
5 Simon and Milo / live in America?
6 Simon / live with Milo?
7 Bertie / a British dog?
8 Bertie / work in America?
9 Eugénie / work for a British magazine?
10 Bertie and Eugénie / live in Paris?

2 Work in pairs. Ask and answer the questions. Use the information in the Reading texts.

1 *Is Milo a police dog? Yes, he is.*

3 Complete the sentences with the correct word.

1 I live *in* / *at* Beijing.
2 I live *for* / *with* my parents.
3 I work *by* / *for* a big company.
4 I work *on* / *in* a factory.
5 I go to work *by* / *for* bus.

Vocabulary

1 Find six technology words in the wordsearch.

i	c	f	w	e	s	t	d	e	r	a	t
h	o	i	s	b	k	o	o	v	m	e	r
t	m	o	b	i	l	e	p	h	o	n	e
y	p	c	a	f	e	m	r	l	u	u	l
w	u	h	a	y	w	a	o	u	s	s	d
r	t	w	e	b	s	i	t	e	e	d	b
f	e	i	n	d	j	l	b	u	i	l	k
m	r	n	i	y	p	r	i	n	t	e	r

2 Match the technology things 1–4 to the words a–d.

1 @ — a email address
2 . — b at
3 / — c dot
4 jim@aol.com — d slash

3 1.84 Listen and (circle) the email address you hear. Repeat the emails.

1 hal006@mail.com — hel06@mail.com
2 sofia@ya.net — sofia@ia.net
3 mercedes@car.com — mercedes@kar.com

Functional language

1 Work in pairs, A and B. You are going to practise saying email addresses and website URLs.

A: Turn to page 116.
B: Turn to page 114.

2 Do you know any other URLs? What are they? Tell a partner.

Speaking

1 Work in small groups. Make questions with the information in the table.

Do you	have		a dog? an email address?
	work/live		in a house? in a flat? next to the school?
	go	(to work) (to school)	by car? by bus?

2 Tell the class three things about your group.

Pablo and Diana live in a house.
Ana goes to work by car, but Ivan goes to work by bus.

Self-assessment (✓)

☐ I can say where I live and work.
☐ I can say email addresses.
☐ I can say website URLs.

6A | Daytime

Grammar: Adverbs of frequency
Vocabulary: Common verbs & nouns (2)
Reading: *Morning people and night people*

VOCABULARY: common verbs & nouns (2)

1 1.85 Match the verbs and phrases in the box to the pictures A–F. Listen and repeat the verbs.

eat   drink   go to bed   wake up   read   sleep

2 Complete the phrases with the verbs from exercise 1.

1 ______ a sandwich/an apple/breakfast
2 ______ water/coffee/tea
3 ______ a newspaper/a book/a magazine

3 Put the verb phrases in the correct order to make a typical Monday morning for you. Tell a partner.

☐ go to work/school
☐ drink coffee/tea/juice/milk
☐ wake up
☐ eat breakfast

On Monday morning I wake up, eat breakfast …

Morning people and night people

When do you like to study? When do you do your best work? Is it in the morning, during daytime or at night?

Different people have different answers for these questions. For example, mornings are always easy for some people. They wake up early. They eat breakfast, they read the newspaper and they go to work on time. These people are morning people.

For other people, mornings are often very difficult. They always go to bed late at night. They sleep late and they wake up late. They sometimes drink a cup of coffee, but they don't eat breakfast (because they are late for work). These are night people.

Some scientists say you don't choose to be a morning person or a night person. It's genetic.

Glossary
on time = not late

READING

1 Read the article above. What is it about, 1, 2 or 3?

1 A typical morning
2 People who prefer mornings and people who prefer evenings
3 When people sleep

Language note

person (singular)   *people* (plural)

2 Read the article again and decide if the sentences are about morning people (☀) or night people (☾).

1 ☀ ☾ Mornings are easy.
2 ☀ ☾ They go to bed late at night.
3 ☀ ☾ They read the morning newspaper.
4 ☀ ☾ They eat breakfast.
5 ☀ ☾ Mornings are difficult.
6 ☀ ☾ They don't eat breakfast.

3 Are you a morning person or a night person? Tell a partner.

GRAMMAR: adverbs of frequency

always *often/usually* *sometimes* *hardly ever* *never*

Use adverbs of frequency to say how often we do something.

*They **always** go to bed late at night.*

Adverbs of frequency go before the main verb.

*They **sometimes** drink a cup of coffee.*

*They don't **often** eat breakfast.*

Adverbs of frequency go after the verb *to be.*

*Mornings are **often** very difficult.*

SEE LANGUAGE REFERENCE PAGE 59

1 Put the words in brackets in the correct place in the sentences.

1 Mike works on Saturday morning. (*always*)
2 He goes to bed late on Friday night. (*sometimes*)
3 He hears the alarm clock. (*hardly ever*)
4 He is tired. (*always*)
5 He eats a big breakfast. (*usually*)
6 He is late for work. (*often*)

2 1.86 Listen and check your answers in exercise 1. Repeat the sentences.

3 Change the sentences in exercise 1 so that they are true for you.

PRONUNCIATION: /e/,/ʌ/,/uː/ & /ɪ/

1 1.87 Listen and repeat the sounds and words.

/e/ never, bed
/ʌ/ sometimes, up
/uː/ juice, usually
/ɪ/ difficult, it

2 1.88 Listen and repeat the sentences.

1 It's a typical morning for Lynne.
2 She usually has juice.
3 Her friend Ed is still in bed.
4 Ed never gets up early.
5 On Sundays, he sometimes doesn't wake up before one.

FUNCTIONAL LANGUAGE: telling the time (1)

1 1.89 Listen and repeat the dialogue.

A: What time is it?
B: It's eight thirty.

Language note

am = in the morning
pm = in the afternoon/evening

SEE LANGUAGE REFERENCE PAGE 59

2 1.90 Listen and underline the times you hear.

1 *8.15pm / 8.50pm*
2 *7 o'clock in the morning / 7 o'clock in the evening*
3 *9.20am / 9.20pm*
4 *12.35 / 12.25*

3 What time is it? Work in pairs. Ask and answer the question with these times.

1 10.00am 3 1.25pm 5 12.15am
2 12.50am 4 4.00pm 6 3.45pm

SPEAKING

1 Complete the sentences so that they are true for you.

On Monday I usually wake up at …
On Sunday I usually wake up at …
I *use / don't use* an alarm clock.
I *usually / sometimes / never* watch TV late at night.
I am *usually / sometimes / always* tired at 11.00pm.
I usually go to bed at …

2 Work in pairs. Tell your partner about you.

3 Change pairs and repeat the exercise.

6B | Free time

Grammar: Present simple (4) (*wh-* questions)
Vocabulary: Common verbs & nouns (3); Free time activities
Reading: Community centre noticeboard

READING & VOCABULARY: common verbs & nouns (3); free time activities

1 Work in pairs. Read the different notices above. Underline the verbs. What are these verbs in your language?

2 Complete the sentences with a verb from exercise 1.

1 On Saturday mornings I _____ football in the park.
2 I don't _____ chess.
3 Many people in my country _____ English at evening classes.
4 I _____ TV at night.
5 I know how to _____ salsa.
6 I _____ sports.

3 1.91 Listen to the recording to check your answers.

4 Make the sentences in exercise 2 true for you.

LISTENING

1 1.92 Listen to a person phoning the Community Centre. Tick (✓) the free time activities she asks about.

1 chess __
2 golf __
3 reading __
4 language class __
5 dance class __

2 1.92 Listen again. Underline the correct answers.

1 The *chess club / dance class* meets on Saturdays.
2 It's at ten o'clock *in the morning / at night.*
3 It's *eight pounds / five pounds* for the month.
4 The language school phone number is *9013 / 9023*.

Language note

£1 (pound) = 100 pence (p)

GRAMMAR: present simple (4) (*wh-* questions)

Who, what, where, when and *how* are question words. Put them in front of the auxiliary verb.
***What** do you do in your free time?*
***When** do you play football?*

SEE LANGUAGE REFERENCE PAGE 58

1 Read the dialogue and complete with words and phrases from the box.

how much when where who what

A: (1) ____ do you do after work?
B: I have a Chinese class.
A: Really? (2) ____ do you learn Chinese?
B: At the Community Centre.
A: (3) ____ is the class?
B: 6.30pm.
A: (4) ____ do you go with?
B: My friend Mike.
A: (5) ____ does it cost?
B: It's free.

2 1.93 Listen to the recording to check your answers. Work in pairs. Read the dialogue.

3 Make questions from the prompts.

1 When / you have free time?
When do you have free time?
2 Where / you live?
3 Where / you work?
4 What / you do in your free time?
5 Where / you go in your free time?

PRONUNCIATION: connected speech (1)

1 1.94 Listen to the questions in Grammar exercise 3. Notice how some words are linked together.

When do‿you have free time?

2 1.95 Listen and repeat.

free time
have free time
you have free time
do you have free time
When do you have free time?

3 Repeat with the other questions in Grammar exercise 3.

4 Work in pairs. Ask and answer the questions in Grammar exercise 3.

When do you have free time?
On Saturday and Sunday.

FUNCTIONAL LANGUAGE: telling the time (2)

1 1.96 Listen and repeat the times.

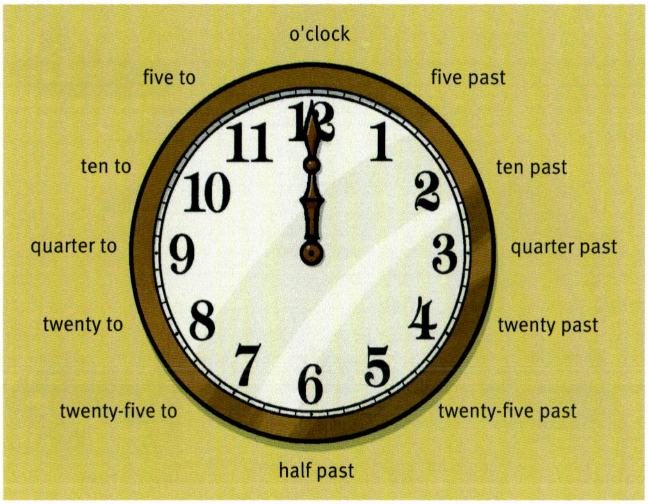

Language note

at + times (*at six o'clock, at half past two*)

2 1.97 Listen and repeat the dialogue.

A: What time is the English class?
B: It's at a quarter past six.

3 Work in pairs. Make other questions about the activities at the Community Centre on page 52.

A: What time is …?
B: It's at …

SPEAKING

1 Work in pairs, A and B.

A: You are a famous person (you decide who).
B: Interview A. Use the questions in Grammar exercise 3.

2 Swap roles and repeat.

6c | Meal time

Grammar: Present simple + *how often* + time expressions
Vocabulary: Food (2) & meals; Food labels
Reading: *Eating habits survey*

Vocabulary & speaking: food (2) & meals

1 2.1 Listen and repeat the food words.

eggs

toast

fruit

milk

soup

chicken

meat

fish

pasta

salad

ice cream

vegetables

2 Complete the sentences with food words.

1 I often have _____ for breakfast.
2 I usually have _____ for lunch.
3 I never have _____ for dinner.
4 I like _____, but I don't like _____.

> *Language note*
>
> With food and drink we can use the verb *have*.
> *have* = *eat* or *drink*
> *I have coffee.* = *I drink coffee.*
> *I have fish.* = *I eat fish.*

3 Make questions from the prompts.

1 What time / have breakfast?
2 What / have for breakfast?
3 What time / have lunch?
4 What / have for lunch?
5 What time / have dinner?
6 What / have for dinner?

4 Work in pairs. Ask and answer the questions in exercise 3.

Reading & listening

1 Look at the *Eating habits survey*. It's difficult to see some of the words. What words are missing?

EATING HABITS SURVEY

1 Do you have three meals a d[illegible]?
☐ YES ☐ NO

2 Do you e[illegible] fruit and/or vegetables every day?
☐ YES ☐ NO

3 Do you eat meat and/or f[illegible] every day?
☐ YES ☐ NO

4 How often do you have a meal at a rest[illegible]?
____

5 How often do you eat with your fam[illegible]?
____

6 How often do you have lunch at work/sc[illegible]?
____

2 2.2 Listen to check your answers.

3 2.2 Listen again and match the answers a–f to the questions 1–6 in Reading exercise 1.

a Well … I eat at home on Friday, but the other days I eat at work. So four times a week.
b We have dinner together every night.
c Do you mean like breakfast, lunch and dinner? Yes, I do.
d Three, maybe four times a year.
e No, I don't. My wife is a vegetarian. I eat meat once a week, maybe.
f Yes, I do. I eat an apple every day.

GRAMMAR: present simple + *how often* + time expressions

Use the present simple to talk about habits and routines.
Use *how often* to ask about habits and routines.

__How often__ do you have coffee?

Use expressions of time to talk about habits.

every/once a/twice a/three times a day/week/month
never

Note: The word *never* goes **before** the verb.

I __never__ have breakfast.

SEE LANGUAGE REFERENCE PAGE 58

1 Complete the diagram with the time expressions from the box.

twice a week every month every year
three times a month ~~never~~ ~~every day~~
once a week

2 Complete the questions in the surveys with verbs from the box.

have ~~see~~ talk go sleep wake

FAMILY HABITS

How often do you ...

(1) *see* your grandparents/children?
(2) ____ lunch with your family?
(3) ____ on the phone with your mother?

SLEEPING HABITS

How often do you ...

(4) ____ up after 11.00am?
(5) ____ to bed after midnight?
(6) ____ eight hours?

3 Work in pairs. Ask the questions in exercise 2. Answer with a time expression from the grammar box.

A: How often do you see your grandparents?
B: Twice a month.

SPEAKING

1 Work in groups of three or four. Create your own healthy living survey. Make questions. Use the surveys in the lesson to help you.

2 Do the survey in your group.

3 Present your results to the class.

Language note

One person ... *Three people ...*
Two people ... *Nobody ...*

ENGLISH AROUND YOU: food labels

1 2.3 Read and listen to the English words from food labels. What are they in your language?

2 Work in pairs. Do food labels in your country use English words? If yes, what words?

6D | Review

Speaking

1 Work in pairs. Say at what time you usually do these things.

I usually wake up at a quarter past seven.

2 Work with a new partner. Ask and answer questions about the activities.

What time do you usually wake up?

Grammar

1 Look at the table and make sentences about Morning Meg or Nighttime Nick.

	go to bed late	wake up early	have breakfast	be late for work
Morning Meg	never	always	every day	hardly ever
Nighttime Nick	always	hardly ever	sometimes	three times a week

2 Match the question words 1–5 to the answers a–e.

1 What?   a Coldplay!
2 Who?   b Free!
3 Where?   c The Ritz Hotel.
4 When?   d Nine o'clock.
5 How much?   e A concert.

3 2.4 Listen to check your answers. Make a similar dialogue.

Vocabulary & listening

1 Complete the menus with the missing food words.

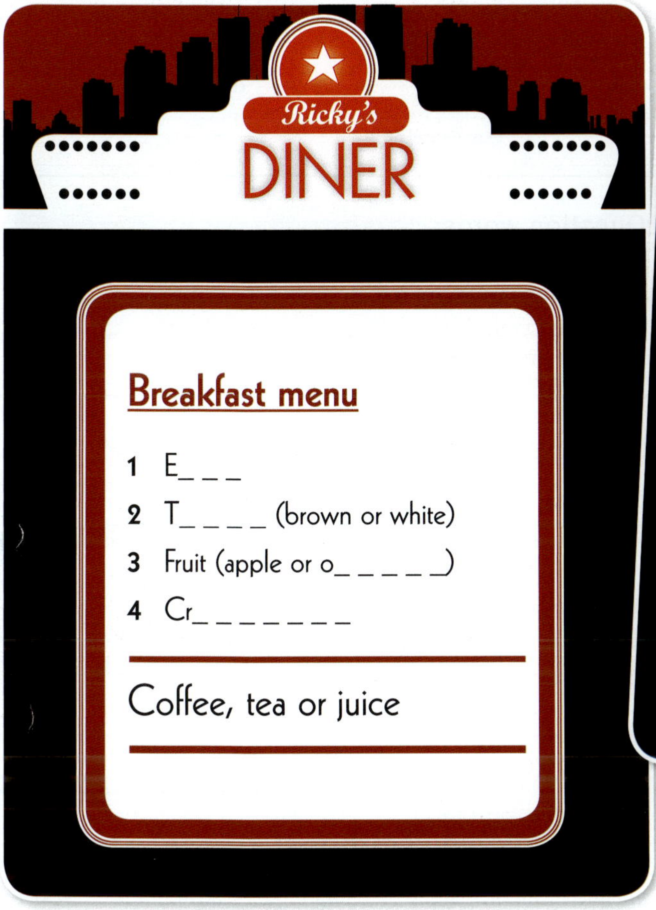

2 2.5 Listen to check your answers.

3 2.6 Listen to a dialogue in Ricky's Diner. Is it morning or afternoon?

4 2.6 Listen again and tick (✓) the food the man would like.

Useful language

What would you like for lunch/breakfast?
I'd like …
Would you like … or …?
… please.
Here you are.

Speaking

1 Work in pairs, A and B.

A: You are the waiter at Ricky's Diner. Ask what B would like for lunch/breakfast.
B: You are a customer at Ricky's Diner. Say what you would like.

Self-assessment (✓)

☐ I can ask the time.
☐ I can tell the time.
☐ I can say what I do on a typical morning.
☐ I know basic food vocabulary.

Grammar

Present simple

The form of the verb is the same except for he/she/it. For *he/she/it*, add *-s*.

affirmative		
I	live	
He/She/It	lives	in New York.
You/We/They	live	

Spelling: present simple verbs with *she/he/it*
For most verbs: add *-s*.

work – works   *eat – eats*   *like – likes*
play – plays

For verbs ending in consonant + *y*: *-y* ➔ *-ies*.

study – studies

For verbs ending in *-ch, -sh, -o*: add *-es*.

do – does   *watch – watches*

Have is an irregular verb.

have		
I	have	
He/She/It	has	a computer.
You/We/They	have	

Make the negative with *don't* + infinitive or *doesn't* (for *she/he/it*) + infinitive.

negative			
I	don't		
He/She/It	doesn't	live	alone.
You/We/They	don't		

For questions, put *do/does* before the subject and the infinitive after the subject.

question		
Do	I	
Does	he/she/it	work?
Do	you/we/they	

Answer these questions with short answers.

Do you speak English?   *Yes, I do.*
Does he have a big family?   *No, he doesn't.*

short answer		
	I	do.
		don't.
Yes,	he/she/it	does.
No,		doesn't.
	you/we/they	do.
		don't.

Question words

What, where, when, who, why and *how* are question words. Put them at the beginning of the question.

How are you?
Where are you from?
What is his name?
Who does she work with?
Why do you like your job?

And, but

And and *but* are conjunctions. Use them to link words, phrases or clauses.

And gives more information.

I have a computer ***and*** *I use it.*

But shows a contrast.

We have a fax machine, ***but*** *we don't use it.*

Adverbs of frequency

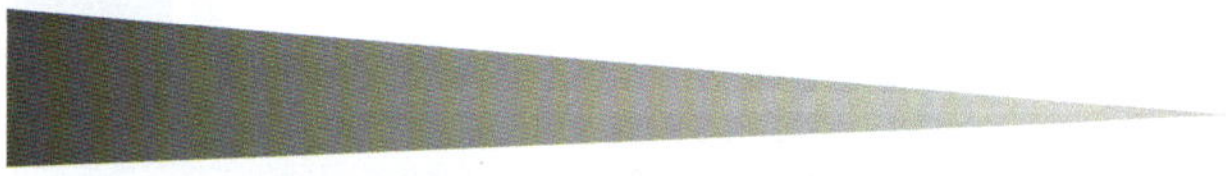

always   *often/usually*   *sometimes*   *hardly ever*   *never*

Use adverbs of frequency to say how often we do something.

They ***always*** *go to bed late at night.*

Adverbs of frequency go before the main verb.

They ***sometimes*** *drink a cup of coffee.*

Adverbs of frequency go after the verb *to be*.

Mornings are ***often*** *very difficult.*

To ask about frequency, use *How often …?*

How often *do you go to bed late?*

We can also use expressions of frequency to talk about how often we do things.

every
once a   *day/week/month*
twice a
three times a

These usually go at the end of a sentence.

I eat fish ***once a week****.*

Functional language

Emails

What's your email address?

@	*at*
.	*dot*
/	*slash*
com	*com*

Telling the time

What time is it?

It's + time

Word list

Common verbs & nouns

bus *n* ***	/bʌs/
company *n* ***	/ˈkʌmp(ə)ni/
dance *v****	/dɑːns/
drink *v****	/drɪŋk/
eat *v****	/iːt/
factory *n* ***	/ˈfæktri/
go *v* ***	/gəʊ/
have *v* ***	/hæv/
hear *v* ***	/ˈhɪə(r)/
like *v* ***	/laɪk/
live *v* ***	/lɪv/
office *n* ***	/ˈɒfɪs/
play *v* ***	/pleɪ/
read *v* ***	/riːd/
school *n*	/skuːl/
shop *n* ***	/ʃɒp/
sleep *v* ***	/sliːp/
taxi *n* ***	/ˈtæksi/
train *n*	/treɪn/
wake up *v*	/ˌweɪk ˈʌp/
work *v* ***	/wɜː(r)k/

Technology

computer *n* ***	/kəmˈpjuːtə(r)/
digital camera *n*	/ˌdɪdʒɪt(ə)l ˈkæm(ə)rə/
email address *n*	/ˈiːmeɪl əˌdres/
fax machine *n*	/ˈfæks məˌʃiːn/
mobile phone *n* **	/ˌməʊbaɪl, ˌməʊb(ə)l ˈfəʊn/
mp3 player *n*	/empiːˈθriː ˈpleɪə/
printer *n* **	/ˈprɪntə(r)/
website *n* **	/ˈwebˌsaɪt/
cancel	/ˈkæns(ə)l/
game console *n*	/ˌgeɪm ˈkɒnsəʊl/
load *v* **	/ləʊd/
save *v* ***	/seɪv/
tablet computer *n*	/ˈtæblət kəmˌpjuːtə(r)/
webcam *n*	/ˈwebkæm/

Adjectives

bad *adj* ***	/bæd/
boring *adj* **	/ˈbɔːrɪŋ/
difficult *adj* ***	/ˈdɪfɪk(ə)lt/
easy *adj* ***	/ˈiːzi/
good *adj* ***	/gʊd/
hard *adj* ***	/hɑː(r)d/
interesting *adj* ***	/ˈɪntrəstɪŋ/

Free time activities

basketball *n* *	/ˈbɑːskɪtˌbɔːl/
chess *n* *	/tʃes/
football *n* ***	/ˈfʊtˌbɔːl/
golf *n* ***	/gɒlf/
rock *n* *	/rɒk/
salsa *n*	/ˈsalsə/
swing *n*	/swɪŋ/
tango *n*	/ˈtaŋgəʊ/
tennis *n* **	/ˈtenɪs/

Food & meals

breakfast *n* ***	/ˈbrekfəst/
chicken *n* **	/ˈtʃɪkɪn/
dinner *n* ***	/ˈdɪnə(r)/
eggs *n* ***	/egz/
fish *n* ***	/fɪʃ/
fruit *n* ***	/fruːt/
ice cream *n* *	/ˈaɪs ˌkriːm/
lunch *n* ***	/lʌntʃ/
meat *n* ***	/miːt/
milk *n* ***	/mɪlk/
pasta *n* *	/ˈpæstə/
salad *n* **	/ˈsæləd/
soup *n* **	/suːp/
toast *n* *	/təʊst/
vegetables *n* ***	/ˈvedʒtəb(ə)lz/

Other words & phrases

afternoon *n* ***	/ˌɑːftə(r)ˈnuːn/
Chinese *adj*	/ˌtʃaɪˈniːz/
choose *v* ***	/tʃuːz/
community centre *n*	/kəˈmjuːnəti ˌsentə(r)/
early *adj* ***	/ˈɜː(r)li/
evening *n* ***	/ˈiːvnɪŋ/
expert *n* ***	/ˈekspɜː(r)t/
flat *n* ***	/flæt/
genetic *adj* **	/dʒəˈnetɪk/
language *n* ***	/ˈlæŋgwɪdʒ/
late *adj, adv* ***	/leɪt/
morning *n* ***	/ˈmɔː(r)nɪŋ/
night *n* ***	/naɪt/
nighttime *n*	/ˈnaɪtˌtaɪm/
nobody *prn* ***	/ˈnəʊbɒdi/
on foot *phrase*	/ˌɒn ˈfʊt/
people *n* ***	/ˈpiːp(ə)l/
person *n* ***	/ˈpɜː(r)s(ə)n/
scientist *n* ***	/ˈsaɪəntɪst/
secretary *n* ***	/ˈsekrətri/
special *adj* ***	/ˈspeʃ(ə)l/
super *adj* **	/ˈsuːpə(r)/
survey *n* ***	/ˈsɜː(r)veɪ/
train *n* ***	/treɪn/
welcome *adj* **	/ˈwelkəm/

7A | City break

Grammar: *There is/there are* (1)
Vocabulary: Places in a city (1)
Reading: *Take a break in the world's top cities*

VOCABULARY: places in a city (1)

1 Match the words 1–12 to the signs A–L.

1 a train station	5 a park	9 a beach
2 an airport	6 a castle	10 tourist information
3 a museum	7 a bridge	11 a bank
4 a hotel	8 a river	12 a taxi

2 2.7 Listen to the recording to check your answers. Repeat the words.

3 Make sentences about your city. Use the words in exercise 1.

PRONUNCIATION: word stress (2)

1 2.8 Listen to the words and the stress patterns. Say the words.

□	□ ▫	▫ □
train park	castle river airport	correct weekend thirteen

2 Put the words from the box in the correct column in exercise 1.

station hotel city police bridge beach bank taxi

3 2.9 Listen and check your answers. Say the words.

READING

1 Look at the magazine page on page 61. What do you know about these cities?

2 Complete the magazine page with the headings below for each city.

Where to stay Getting there Things to see and do

3 Read the magazine page again. Mark the sentences *B* for Barcelona and *P* for Prague.

1 ______ There are beaches.
2 ______ There's a river.
3 ______ There's a train to the airport.
4 ______ There's a museum with Picasso art.
5 ______ There's a Mozart music show.
6 ______ There's an old bridge.
7 ______ There's a castle.

4 Work in pairs. Do you know Barcelona or Prague? Would you like to visit these cities for a weekend break? Why or why not?

GRAMMAR: *there is/there are* (1)

Use *there is/there are* to talk about the existence of things.
There is + *a/an* + singular noun
There is *an airport.*
There are + plural noun
There are *buses from the airport to the city.*

SEE LANGUAGE REFERENCE PAGE 76

1 Underline the correct word to complete the sentences.

In the classroom …
1 there *is* / *are* 20 students.
2 there *is* / *are* a teacher.
3 there *is* / *are* three windows.
4 there *is* / *are* one door.
5 there *is* / *are* 30 desks.

2 2.10 Listen to check your answers. Repeat the words. Make the sentences true for your classroom.

CITY BREAK MAGAZINE

Take a break in the world's top cities

BARCELONA – The Spanish city is the PERFECT place for a weekend break.

City beaches

______

There's a train every 40 minutes from the airport to Barcelona Sants train station. Taxis are 25–30 euros from the airport to the city.

______

There are many hotels in the city centre. Email our office for information.

______

There are lots of things to do in Barcelona. Go for a walk on the famous Ramblas. See the Sagrada Familia church and other buildings by the architect Gaudi. If you like art, go to the Picasso Museum in the old part of town. Watch a Barcelona football match in the city stadium Camp Nou. Barcelona is a Mediterranean city and there are beautiful beaches in and next to the city.

Sagrada Familia church

PRAGUE – Wake up in the BEAUTIFUL capital of the Czech Republic.

Charles Bridge

______

There's an international airport next to the city and taxis are 600 CZ. There are also buses at the airport.

______

Stay in Prague's beautiful hotels in the city centre. You can also stay in one of the old apartments near the river. Email our office for more details.

______

Look at the statues on Charles Bridge. Go for a walk in the old city and next to the beautiful River Vltava. See Prague Castle, one of the oldest castles in Europe. For music lovers, there is a puppet show of Mozart's opera *The Magic Flute*.

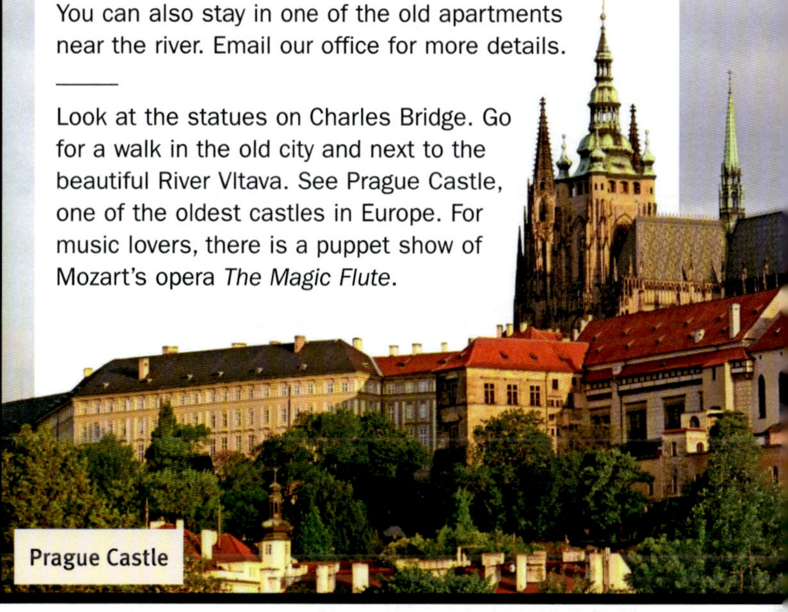
Prague Castle

3 Look at the information about St Petersburg, Russia. Make sentences with *There is/There are* and the words in **bold**.

There is an international airport.
There are buses and taxis.

ST PETERSBURG

Getting there

Pulkovo-2 international **airport**
Buses and taxis to city centre

Where to stay

Hotels and apartments in the city centre

Things to see and do

The Peter and Paul **Cathedral**
The (more than 300) **bridges** of St Petersburg
The Mikhailovsky **Castle**
Beautiful **parks** in Pushkin
The Hermitage **Museum**
The Summer **Palace**

SPEAKING

1 Prepare a short presentation about a city you know. Use the phrases below to help you.

COME FOR A WEEKEND CITY BREAK IN ______

Getting here

It's in …
There's an airport/train station.

Where to stay

There are hotels …

Things to do and see

Go for a walk (in the old town/ in the city centre/on the beach).
See the …
There's a …
There are …

2 Work in pairs. Present your weekend city break to your partner.

7B | City life

Grammar: *There is/there are* (2) (questions & negative)
Vocabulary: Adjectives (2); Places in a city (2)
Reading & listening: Dialogue about a neighbourhood

Speaking

1 Look at the picture of Lemmington. Work in pairs and make sentences.

There's a river. *There are two parks.*

Vocabulary: adjectives (2); places in a city (2)

1 2.11 Read and listen to someone talk about Lemmington. What are the words in **bold** in your language?

It's a **small** city.
It's **beautiful**.
Public transport is **cheap**.
The people are **friendly**.

2 Match the words in **bold** in exercise 1 to the opposites below.

1 ugly
2 big
3 unfriendly
4 expensive

3 2.12 Listen to the recording to check your answers. Make the sentences in exercise 1 true for your city.

4 2.13 Find these places on the map. Listen and repeat the words.

a shop
a hospital
a market
a supermarket
a bank

Reading & listening

1 2.14 Mr and Mrs Walker (Mr and Mrs W) are at the Lemmington Estate Agency speaking to the estate agent (EA). Read and listen to the dialogue. What is the problem?

Mr W: I'm Jeremy Walker. This is my wife, Annie. We're here about the flat.
EA: Ah yes. Nice to meet you. Well, Mr Walker, we have the perfect flat for you.
Mr W: Oh. Is it near the city centre? We love city life.
EA: Near the city centre? It's in the city centre!
Mrs W: We have two small children. Are there any schools in the area?
EA: Oh yes, there are three schools.
Mrs W: Is there a park?
EA: Yes, there is. In fact, there are two parks. This is a good neighbourhood for children.
Mr W: And a hospital? Is there a hospital?
EA: Yes, there is. Look, there's a hospital here. Next to the river.
Mrs W: Oh, that's good.
EA: There's also a market and there are very nice shops. And public transport is very good and cheap here, too.
Mrs W: Jeremy, this is wonderful!
Mr W: One more question, how old is the flat?
EA: Err … just a minute. It's … it's 95 years old.
Mrs W: What? Ninety-five?
EA: Yes, well …
Mr W: Look! Your website says *new* houses and flats.
EA: But it's very cheap.
Both: No, thank you. Goodbye.

Glossary
neighbourhood *n* a particular area of a town

2 Read the dialogue in exercise 1 again and decide if the sentences are true (T) or false (F). Correct the false sentences.

1 The flat is in the city centre.
2 There are three schools.
3 There are three parks.
4 There isn't a hospital.
5 Public transport is cheap.
6 The flat is new.

GRAMMAR: *there is/there are* (2) (questions & negative)

Negative
Use *not* (*n't*).
There is a school.
*There **isn't** a school.*

Question
Change the verb and the subject.
There is a hospital.
***Is there** a hospital?* *Yes, there is.*
No, there isn't.

Use *any* with plural nouns in questions and negatives.
*There aren't **any** discos.*
*Are there **any** schools?* *Yes, there are.*
No, there aren't.

SEE LANGUAGE REFERENCE PAGE 76

1 Rewrite the sentences. Use the symbols in brackets ().

1 There is a school. (?)
Is there a school?
2 There are shops. (–)
There aren't any shops.
3 There is a bank. (?)
4 There are parks. (?)
5 There are buses. (–)
6 There isn't a hospital. (?)
7 There aren't any shops. (+)
8 Are there any museums? (–)

2 Work in pairs. Ask and answer questions about your neighbourhood.

1 any shops?
Are there any shops? Yes, there are./No, there aren't.
2 a hospital?
3 a train station?
4 any beaches?
5 a hotel?
6 a bank?
7 any schools?
8 a market?

SPEAKING

1 Work in pairs, A and B.

A: Turn to page 115.
B: Turn to page 116.

Find three differences in your pictures.

'And this is the sitting room and the bedroom, and the toilet, and…'

7c | City tour

Vocabulary: Travel words; Signs
Functional language: Survival English
Listening: In the city of York

Listening

1 Read the information at the bottom of the page about the city of York.

2 2.15 Listen to four dialogues. Match the dialogues 1–4 to the photos A–D.

A

B

C

D

3 2.15 Listen again. Choose the correct answer.

Dialogue 1
a) The city tour is at 4.45.
b) The city tour is at 3.45.

Dialogue 2
a) There are tickets for the Mystery Play tonight.
b) There aren't any tickets for the Mystery Play tonight.

Dialogue 3
a) The woman is from York.
b) The woman isn't from York.

Dialogue 4
a) They are near the castle.
b) They aren't near the castle.

Functional language: survival English

1 2.16 Listen and complete the phrases.

I'm (1) s_____, I don't (2) sp_____ English.
I don't (3) u_____.
I only speak a (4) l_____ English.
Can you repeat, (5) p_____?
Do you (6) s_____ German?

2 2.16 Listen again and repeat the phrases.

3 Look at audioscript 2.15 on page 123. Underline examples of the phrases.

4 Work in pairs. Choose one of the dialogues from Listening exercise 2 and practise.

The city of York is in the North of England. York is famous for its Roman and Viking history, and it is a popular destination for tourists.

VOCABULARY: travel words

1 Work in pairs. Match the words 1–7 to the photos A–F. Use a dictionary to help you.

1 a map
2 a passport
3 luggage
4 a ticket (single/return)
5 a phrase book
6 a visa
7 money

2 2.17 Listen to check your answers. Say the words.

3 Imagine you are on a three-day holiday in Britain. Underline five things you'd like to take with you.

a passport
a car
a visa
a bag
an English phrase book
a guide book for Britain
British money
a map
an identity card
a digital camera
a credit card

4 Work in pairs. Compare your lists.

I'd like to take a map, a visa, British money …

PRONUNCIATION: /m/, /f/, /v/ & /p/

1 2.18 Listen and repeat the sounds and words.

/m/ money
/f/ four
/v/ visa
/p/ passport

2 2.19 Listen and repeat the sentences.

1 My mother makes money at the market.
2 Fiona has forty-four favourite phrases in French.
3 Vincent needs a visa to visit the Vatican.
4 Peter uses public transport in Paris.

SPEAKING

1 Work in pairs, A and B.

A: You are a tourist in New York City, US. You only speak a little English.
Turn to page 116.
B: You work at tourist information in Manhattan.
Turn to page 115.

ENGLISH AROUND YOU: signs

1 Look at these signs in English. What do these words mean in your language?

2 2.20 Listen and repeat the words.

3 Are there any signs in English in your city? What do they say?

7D | Review

Speaking & vocabulary

1 Work in pairs. Think of examples of ...

- a small city.
- a big, ugly city.
- a good, cheap restaurant.
- an expensive restaurant.
- a beautiful, old castle.

2 Work with another pair. Read your examples. Can the other students guess the category?

Grammar

1 The dialogue is missing six examples of *there*. Where do they go? The first one has been done for you.

A: Can I help you?

B: I'd like some information about your hotel.

A: Yes, of course. What would you like to know?

B: Is *there* a restaurant?

A: Yes, is. are two restaurants in the hotel.

B: Two restaurants. Thank you. Is a swimming pool?

A: No, I'm sorry, isn't.

B: Oh. No swimming pool. OK. Is the hotel in the city centre?

A: No, it isn't. We are fifteen kilometres from the city centre. But are trains and taxis. And we are very close to the airport.

B: Good. Thank you very much.

A: You're welcome.

2 2.21 Listen to the recording to check your answers.

Listening

1 Match the words in the box to the photos A–E.

a phrase book	a passport	
money	a map	luggage

A

B

C

D

E

2 2.22 Listen to four dialogues. Match the dialogues 1–4 to the photos A–E in exercise 1. There is one extra photo.

Speaking

THE CITY GAME

1 Work in groups of three or four. Play *The City Game*. You need counters  and some dice .

1 Choose a city you know and write the name in the space.

2 You are all in the city. One person works at Tourist Information. The others are tourists.

3 The person at Tourist Information puts their counter in the middle.

4 The tourists put their counters on START. One tourist starts. The tourist rolls the dice and moves along the board.

5 If you land on a question square, ask the question to Tourist Information. Start your question *Excuse me …?* Tourist Information gives an answer.

6 If you land on a  square, it is the next player's turn.

7 If you land on a  square, change places with Tourist Information.

8 When you finish, it is the next player's turn.

9 Repeat stages 4–8 until all players finish.

Self-assessment (✓)

☐ I can talk about where I live.
☐ I can say when I don't understand.
☐ I can ask for help in English.

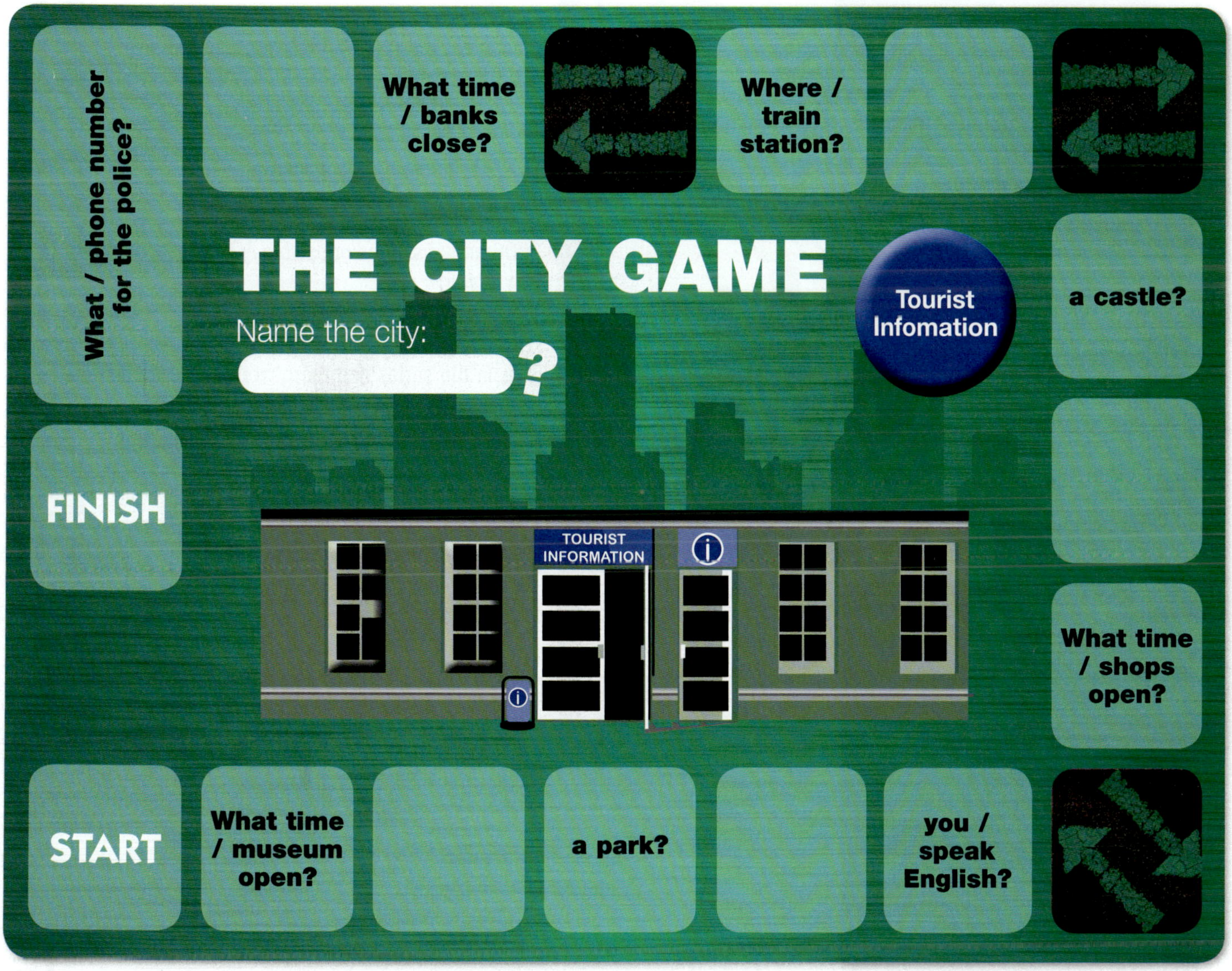

8A | Film sequels

Grammar: *Was/were*
Vocabulary: Years
Reading: *Do it again*

Speaking

1 Work in pairs. Look at the posters of old television shows and films. Do you know them? Tell your partner.

Reading

1 Read the magazine article and match the posters A–C in Speaking exercise 1 to the television shows or films. There is one film with no poster. Which one is it?

DO IT AGAIN

The number one rule in television and film is 'if it works, do it again'. Remakes and sequels are big business in Hollywood. Today we look at some of the most famous film franchises in Hollywood.

Batman was originally a comic book from 1939. There are now ten films about the character. The first *Batman* film was in 1943 and the last one was *The Dark Knight Rises* in 2012. There are also television shows and very popular video games about the character.

The *Mission: Impossible* films with Tom Cruise (*Mission: Impossible I* was in 1996, *Mission: Impossible II* in 2000, *Mission: Impossible III* in 2006 and *Mission: Impossible IV* in 2011) were very popular.'

The first James Bond film was *Dr No*, in 1962. For the next 45 years there were 21 more films in the series and there were six actors in the role of the British secret agent.

But one of the most popular film franchises is *Star Wars*. The first *Star Wars* film was in 1977. There were more *Star Wars* films in 1980 and 1983. The next three films in the *Star Wars* franchise were in 1999, 2002 and 2005. There was also a cartoon film and television show.

2 Read the article again. Complete the sentences.

1 ______ are good for business in Hollywood.
2 ______ was a comic book.
3 ______ was a television show in the 1960s.
4 The first ______ was in 1977.

3 Do you know the Hollywood remakes and sequels from the article? Do you like them? Tell a partner.

GRAMMAR: *was/were*

The past simple of *to be* is *was/were.*
The Mission: Impossible *films* **were** *very popular.*
The first James Bond *film* **was** *in 1962.*
I/He/She/It *was*
You/We/They *were*

SEE LANGUAGE REFERENCE PAGE 76

1 2.23 Listen and put the sentences in the past simple.

1 The film is at seven o'clock.
2 The tickets are expensive.
3 You are on the street.
4 It is cold.
5 I am late.
6 You are angry.

2 Complete the texts about television shows and films with the verb *to be* in the past simple.

1 The first James Bond film ______ *Dr No* (1962). The actor Sean Connery ______ James Bond.
2 *Bewitched* ______ a television show from the 1960s. Nicole Kidman was in the 2005 Hollywood remake.
3 The original *Star Trek* ______ on television from 1966 to 1969.
4 The American television shows *The X-Files* and *Friends* ______ very popular in the 1990s.
5 *The Lord of the Rings* ______ a book by JRR Tolkein before it ______ a series of Hollywood films.

VOCABULARY & PRONUNCIATION: years

1 2.24 Listen and repeat the years.

2008	two thousand and eight
2000	two thousand
1954	nineteen fifty-four
2010	two thousand and ten
1960s	the nineteen sixties

2 Work in pairs. Say these years.

1	1889	5	1962
2	1984	6	1977
3	1926	7	2014
4	2009	8	1930

3 2.25 Listen and complete the sentences with a year from exercise 2. When were they born?

1 Marilyn Monroe
2 Charlie Chaplin
3 Jodie Foster
4 Clint Eastwood
5 Orlando Bloom
6 Scarlett Johansson

was born in …

4 Work in pairs. Repeat the sentences in exercise 3.

SPEAKING

1 2.26 Read and listen to the text.

I'm a child of the nineties

I was born in the eighties. When I was young, my favourite TV shows were *The X-Files* and *The Simpsons*. My favourite actor was Kevin Costner. My favourite singer was Kurt Cobain from Nirvana. There was a picture of my favourite football player Luis Figo on the wall in the bedroom.

2 Work in pairs. Make a similar text about your partner. Don't ask questions, guess.

3 Read your sentences to your partner. Were you correct?

4 Now work with another student. Talk about your partner.

Gabriela is a child of the 1990s. When she was young …

8B | Film script

Grammar: *Was/were* (questions, negative & time expressions)
Vocabulary: Television
Reading: Dialogue from a detective film

READING

1 2.27 Listen and match words from the box to the pictures A–C.

Fire!   Help!   Look out!

2 You are going to read a dialogue from a film script, *Crime Scene*. Check you understand these words.

dead   blood   fingerprints   lawyer   divorced

3 2.28 Read and listen to the dialogue. Answer the questions.

1 What do John Kellerman (JK) and Dana Diaz (DD) do?
2 Does Mr Magnus (Mr M) know Peter Gordon?

JK: Mr Magnus. My name's John Kellerman and this is Dana Diaz. She works with the Crime Scene department.
Mr M: Well, nice to meet you, but I don't know what this is all about. Why am I here?
DD: Mr Magnus, do you know Peter Gordon?
Mr M: Yes, I do. We work at the same factory.
JK: Mr Magnus. I have some bad news. Mr Gordon is … dead.
Mr M: That's impossible! He was at the factory yesterday!
DD: There was a fire at the factory last night, Mr Magnus.
JK: Where were you at eight o'clock last night?
Mr M: Ummm, I was at home.
JK: Really? Were you with somebody? Your wife?
Mr M: No, I wasn't with my wife. I'm divorced.
DD: That's right. Your wife, your ex-wife, was Peter Gordon's new girlfriend.
Mr M: Really?
DD: Mr Magnus, if you were at home, why were your fingerprints on the factory emergency exit?
Mr M: Wh … What?
DD: Yes, your fingerprints. And why was your blood on Mr Gordon's jacket?
Mr M: Listen, I wasn't at the factory last night and I wasn't with Peter.
JK: Mr Magnus. You *were* at the factory. And you *were* with Mr Gordon.
Mr M: I … I …
DD: Do you have a good lawyer, Mr Magnus?

Glossary
emergency exit *n* a door that leads out of a public place when necessary

4 Read the dialogue again and decide if the sentences are true (T) or false (F). Correct the false sentences.

1 Mr Magnus is dead.
2 Mr Magnus works with Peter Gordon.
3 There was a fire at the factory.
4 Mr Magnus wasn't at the factory yesterday.
5 Mr Magnus isn't married.
6 Mr Magnus' blood and fingerprints were at the crime scene.

GRAMMAR: *was/were* (questions, negative & time expressions)

Negative
Add *not* or *n't* to *was/were*.
*I **wasn't** at the factory.*
Question
The verb and the subject change places.
***Were you** at the factory?*
*Where **were you** last night?*
Short answer
Yes, I was. *No, I wasn't.*
Time expressions
You can use these time expressions with the past.
yesterday
last night/week/month
Put them at the beginning or end of a sentence.

SEE LANGUAGE REFERENCE PAGE 76

1 Rearrange the words to make sentences or questions.

1 you friends Were Peter with ?
2 factory at the He yesterday was .
3 fingerprints door Your were the on .
4 night last you were Where ?
5 factory at you the Were ?
6 her last night with wasn't I .

2 2.29 Listen to the recording to check your answers. Repeat the sentences.

3 Make questions with *Where* and words and expressions from the box.

last Friday night last Sunday morning
at 11.15 last night at 5.30 yesterday

4 Work in pairs. Ask and answer the questions in exercise 3.

Where were you last Friday night?
I was at home.

SPEAKING

1 Play *Find someone who ...*

Move around the class. Ask *Were you ...?* questions. Answer *Yes, I was* or *No, I wasn't*. Complete the spaces with names.

A: Were you in bed at nine o'clock last night?
B: Yes, I was.

Find someone who ...

★ ________ was in bed at nine o'clock last night.
★ ________ wasn't in English class last week.
★ ________ wasn't in bed at 6.30 this morning.
★ ________ was at a party last weekend.
★ ________ wasn't at work yesterday.
★ ________ was at the cinema last Saturday or Sunday.

ENGLISH AROUND YOU: television

1 Read the names of famous British/American television shows from recent years. Do you know these shows? Do you like them?

TV GUIDE

1	Big Brother	★★★★
2	Lost	★★★
3	Heroes	★★
4	X Factor	★★★★
5	House	★
6	Grey's Anatomy	★★
7	The Wire	★★★
8	Mad Men	★

2 What are these shows in your language?

3 Which other American or British films/TV shows do you know? What are their names in English?

8c | Film reviews

Grammar: Subject & object pronouns
Vocabulary: Adjectives of opinion
Functional language: Giving an opinion

VOCABULARY: adjectives of opinion

1 Read the three reviews and underline the adjectives.

A

The Golden Dragon

A film from China opens the International Film Festival this week. *The Golden Dragon* has good special effects and the acting isn't bad. But watch out, this film is more than three hours!

B

Robot Attack

★★★★
A great science fiction film!
Roger Dryden, *The Times*

★★★★
VERY, VERY GOOD. THE ACTION DOESN'T STOP!
Duncan Foord,
Independent Daily Newspaper

★★★
I like this film. I like it a lot.
Mercedes Grau, *Latin film press*

C

File Edit View Favourites Tools Help Links »

Customer Review – ***The Promise* (DVD)**

★★☆☆☆

I hate this DVD. It's awful. Don't buy it.

Freddy, January 4, 2012 Buenos Aires, Argentina

2 Complete the table with the adjectives from exercise 1.

PRONUNCIATION: intonation (3)

1 **2.30** Listen to the sentences. Are they positive or negative opinions? Underline the correct symbol.

1
2
3
4

2 **2.30** Listen again and repeat the sentences. Copy the intonation.

LISTENING

1 **2.31** Listen to three people giving their opinions. Which speaker 1–3 talks about one of the films in Vocabulary exercise 1? What do the other speakers talk about?

2 **2.31** Listen again and underline the correct words to complete the sentences.

1 Speaker 1 *likes / doesn't like* the *computers / food.*
2 Speaker 2 *likes / doesn't like* the *film / computers.*
3 Speaker 3 *likes / doesn't like* the *film / food.*

FUNCTIONAL LANGUAGE: giving an opinion

1 **2.32** Listen and repeat.

A: What do you think of the food?
B: I like it.
C: I think it's great.

2 Put the phrases in the box in the correct order on the diagram.

I like it. I don't like it. It's OK.

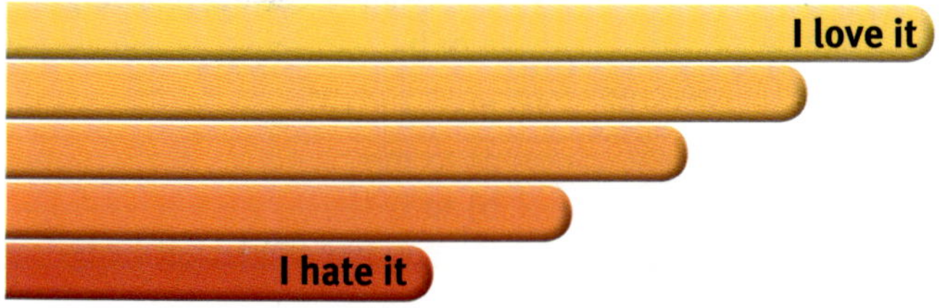

3 Make sentences with words from the box. Use the phrases from exercise 2.

science fiction films football computers rock music cats Chinese food

I like football.
I don't like rock music.
Science fiction films are OK.
I don't like cats.

GRAMMAR: subject & object pronouns

Pronouns have two forms.
Subject pronouns
He *is an actor.*
Object pronouns
I like ***him****.*

SEE LANGUAGE REFERENCE PAGE 76

1 Look at audioscript 2.31 on page 123. Underline all the object pronouns.

2 Replace the underlined words below with object pronouns.

1 Do you like Italian food?
Yes, I love Italian food.
2 Do you like dogs?
Yes, I like dogs.
3 Do you like golf?
No, I hate golf.
4 Do you like mornings?
Yes, I like mornings.
5 Do you like Javier Bardem?
No, I don't like Javier Bardem.
6 Do you like Penélope Cruz?
Yes, I love Penélope Cruz.

3 Work in pairs. Ask the questions in exercise 2. Give your own answers.

SPEAKING

1 Read the instructions to the game.

2 Work in small groups. Play the game.

Game: *That's My Opinion*

1 Complete the circles with names of people or things that you know.
2 Work in small groups.
3 Ask and give opinions.

A: What do you think of Shakira?
B: I love her!
C: I think she's OK.

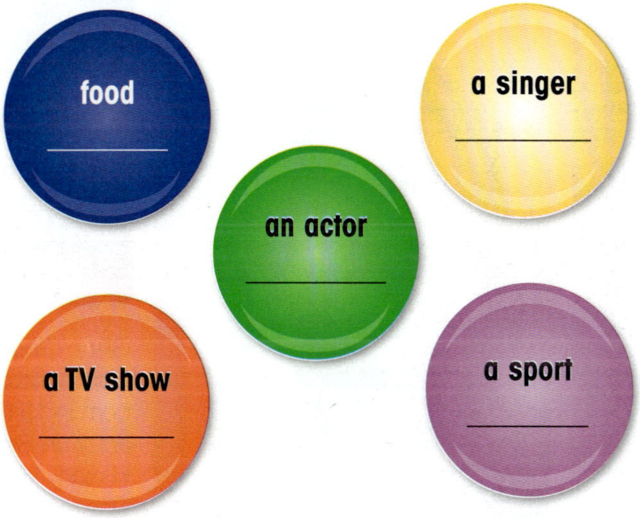

Useful language

What do you think of …?
Do you like …?
I like/love/hate it/him/her/them.
It's OK.
I think it's/he's/she's/they're great/good/bad.

8D Review

Reading

1 Read the article about two actors.

1 Who was on television first, then in films?
2 Who was in films first, then on television?

From TELEVISION to the MOVIES and VICE VERSA

Jennifer Aniston was born in California in 1969. Her mother and father were both actors. Jennifer Aniston got her first big acting role in the television series *Friends* in 1994. It was a very successful television series for ten years. Jennifer Aniston is now a big Hollywood star and was in many blockbuster films.

Glenn Close is from Connecticut, US. She was born in 1947. She was an actor on Broadway and then in many Hollywood films. She was most famous for her roles in *Fatal Attraction and Dangerous Liaisons*. She was nominated many times for film awards like the Oscars™ in the 1980s. Glenn Close is now more famous for her television roles. She was a police chief in the police show *The Shield* (2002–2008) and is a lawyer in the drama show *Damages* (2007–2011).

2 Read the article again and answer the questions about each actor.

1 Where was she born?
2 When was she born?
3 What was her first acting job?

Grammar

1 Choose the correct answer, a or b.

1 Please listen …
a) to me.
b) to I.
2 Do you like the singer Lady Gaga?
a) I don't know she.
b) I don't know her.
3 Does your father speak English?
a) He speaks a little.
b) Him speaks a little.
4 She loves me, but I don't …
a) love she.
b) love her.
5 They know us, but we don't know …
a) them.
b) they.

2 Put the words in the box in the correct order on the diagram.

yesterday	last night
this morning	last Saturday
last week	last March

Vocabulary

1 Underline the correct word to complete the dialogues.

1 **A:** Do you like it?
B: No, I don't. It's *great / awful*.

2 **A:** What do you think?
B: It's *beautiful / ugly*. I love it!

3 **A:** Teacher! Teacher! Look!
B: Very *good / bad*, Barnaby. Everybody, look at Barnaby's work.

4 **A:** How's the weather today, Jim?
B: The weather today isn't very *good / bad*.

2 2.33 Listen to check your answers. Read the dialogues.

Functional language

1 2.34 Read and listen to the text.

Recently, the British Council asked more than 7,000 students of English in 46 countries: what is the most beautiful word in English? Here are the top five words:

2 Do you have a favourite word in English? Complete the sentences with words you know in English.

1 I like the word …
2 I love the word …
3 I don't like the word …
4 I hate the word …

3 Work in pairs. Compare your sentences.

Self-assessment (✓)

- ☐ I can say when and where I was born.
- ☐ I can ask about likes and dislikes.
- ☐ I can talk about things I like and don't like.

7 & 8 Language reference

GRAMMAR

There is/there are

affirmative		
There	is	a supermarket.
	are	two schools.

negative		
There	isn't	a restaurant.
	aren't	any parks.

question			short answer
Is	there	a park?	Yes, there is. No, there isn't.
Are		any parks?	Yes, there are. No, there aren't.

Use *any* with plural nouns in questions and negatives.

There aren't ***any*** *discos.*

Are there ***any*** *schools?* *Yes, there are.*
No, there aren't.

Was/were

The past simple of *to be* is *was/were*.

The Mission: Impossible *films* ***were*** *very popular.*

The first Star Wars *film* ***was*** *in 1977.*

affirmative & negative		
I He/She/It	was wasn't	on television.
You/We/They	were weren't	

question		
Was	I he/she/it	in a film?
Were	you/we/they	

Time expressions

Use these time expressions with the past.

yesterday/last night/week/month

Put them at the beginning or end of a sentence.

- **now**
- **this morning**
- **last night**
- **yesterday**
- **last saturday**
- **last week**
- **last March**
- **last year**

Subject & object pronouns

Pronouns have two forms:

Subject pronouns come before the verb.

He *is an actor.*

Object pronouns come after the verb.

I like ***him****.*

subject	object
I	me
you	you
he	him
she	her
it	it
we	us
they	them

Functional language

Survival English

I'm sorry, I don't speak English.
I don't understand.
I only speak a little English.
Can you repeat, please?
Do you speak German?

Giving an opinion

What do you think of the food?
I think it's great/awful.
I like it.
It's OK.
I don't like it.

Word list

Places in a city

airport *n* ***	/ˈeə(r)ˌpɔː(r)t/
bank *n* ***	/bæŋk/
beach *n* ***	/biːtʃ/
bridge *n* ***	/brɪdʒ/
castle *n* **	/ˈkɑːs(ə)l/
hospital *n* ***	/ˈhɒspɪt(ə)l/
market *n* ***	/ˈmɑː(r)kɪt/
museum *n* ***	/mjuːˈziːəm/
park *n* ***	/pɑː(r)k/
river *n* ***	/ˈrɪvə(r)/
shop *n* ***	/ʃɒp/
supermarket *n* **	/ˈsuːpə(r)ˌmɑː(r)kɪt/
(train) station *n* ***	/(ˈtreɪn ˌsteɪʃ(ə)n) ˈsteɪʃ(ə)n/

Adjectives

awful *adj* **	/ˈɔːf(ə)l/
bad *adj* ***	/bæd/
beautiful *adj* ***	/ˈbjuːtəf(ə)l/
big *adj* ***	/bɪg/
cheap *adj* ***	/tʃiːp/
expensive *adj* ***	/ɪkˈspensɪv/
favourite *adj* **	/ˈfeɪv(ə)rət/
friendly *adj* ***	/ˈfren(d)li/
good *adj* ***	/gʊd/
great *adj* ***	/greɪt/
nice *adj* ***	/naɪs/
original *adj* ***	/əˈrɪdʒ(ə)nəl/
popular *adj* ***	/ˈpɒpjʊlə(r)/
real *adj* ***	/rɪəl/
small *adj* ***	/smɔːl/
ugly *adj* **	/ˈʌgli/
unfriendly *adj* *	/ʌnˈfren(d)li/

Travel words

luggage *n* *	/ˈlʌgɪdʒ/
map *n* ***	/mæp/
money *n* ***	/ˈmʌni/
passport *n* *	/ˈpɑːspɔː(r)t/
phrase book *n*	/ˈfreɪz ˌbʊk/
ticket (single/return) *n* ***	/ˈtɪkɪt (ˈsɪŋg(ə)l, rɪˈtɜː(r)n)/
visa *n* *	/ˈviːzə/

Other words & phrases

actor *n* ***	/ˈæktə(r)/
again *adv* ***	/əˈgen/
bar *n* ***	/bɑː(r)/
blood *n* ***	/blʌd/
break *n* **	/breɪk/
dead *adj* ***	/ded/
desk *n* ***	/desk/
detective *n* **	/dɪˈtektɪv/
divorced *adj* **	/dɪˈvɔː(r)st/
ex-wife *n*	/ˌeks ˈwaɪf/
fingerprint *n*	/ˈfɪŋgə(r)ˌprɪnt/
fire *n* ***	/ˈfaɪə(r)/
impossible *adj* ***	/ɪmˈpɒsəb(ə)l/
lawyer *n* ***	/ˈlɔːjə(r)/
many *det* ***	/ˈmeni/
opera *n* **	/ˈɒp(ə)rə/
parking *n* *	/ˈpɑː(r)kɪŋ/
public transport *n* *	/ˌpʌblɪk ˈtrænspɔː(r)t/
pull *v* ***	/pʊl/
puppet *n*	/ˈpʌpɪt/
push *v* ***	/pʊʃ/
remake n	/ˈriːmeɪk/
scene *n* ***	/siːn/
series *n* ***	/ˈsɪəriːz/
show *v* ***	/ʃəʊ/
statue *n* **	/ˈstætʃuː/
stay *v* ***	/steɪ/
stop *v* ***	/stɒp/
tour *n* **	/tʊə(r)/
wake up *v*	/ˌweɪk ˈʌp/
weekend *n* ***	/ˌwiːkˈend/

9A | Holiday

Grammar: Past simple irregular verbs (affirmative)
Vocabulary: Big numbers
Reading: Email about a holiday

VOCABULARY: big numbers

1 2.35 Read and listen to the facts about India and complete the information with numbers.

2 Match the words 1–7 to the numbers a–g.

1	four hundred	a	400
2	a million	b	1,000
3	a hundred thousand	c	2,500
4	a thousand	d	10,000
5	a billion	e	100,000
6	two thousand five hundred	f	1,000,000
7	ten thousand	g	1,000,000,000

3 2.36 Listen and repeat the numbers.

FACTFILE: INDIA

Population: 1.189 billion

Capital city: New Delhi – population (1) _____ million

Other important cities:
Mumbai (was Bombay) – population (2) _____ million
Calcutta – population (3) _____ million

Languages: Hindi, English and (4) _____ other languages

Currency: 1 rupee = (5) _____ paise

Area: 3,300,000 sq km

READING

1 Read Patti's email. Choose the correct answers a, b or c.

1 This is an email for …
a) Patti's parents.
b) Patti's friends.
c) Patti's work.

2 The email is about …
a) Patti's job.
b) Patti's holiday.
c) Patti's family.

File Edit View Favourites Tools Help Links »

To: d.vora@aol.com
Subject: Last day of our Indian holiday

It's Friday! It's our last day in India and we're in New Delhi! We're fine, this is a quick email to tell you how we are.

Yesterday we were in the city of Agra. We saw the Taj Mahal, of course. It was fantastic, but there were lots of tourists.

New Delhi is very big. The guide book says there are eleven million people here! Today we went shopping in the New Delhi markets. They are beautiful – but very crowded and noisy. We went to the National Museum, but it was closed.

Last night we went to a restaurant with some of Anne's friends. I ate a typical Indian dish, but I don't remember the name now. It had meat in it. I drank some chai last night, too! It's a kind of tea, and very popular here.

Anyway, hope you and Dad are OK. There are many internet cafés here, so send me an email soon.

Love
Patti

2 Read the email again and decide if the sentences are true (T) or false (F). Correct the false sentences.

1 Yesterday they were in New Delhi.
2 There were lots of tourists at the Taj Mahal.
3 They went shopping in New Delhi.
4 The National Museum was closed.
5 Patti doesn't eat meat.

GRAMMAR: past simple irregular verbs (affirmative)

1 Find the past simple of the verbs in the email on page 78 and complete the table.

Present	**Past**
go	*went*
see	______
eat	______
drink	______
have	______

SEE LANGUAGE REFERENCE PAGE 94

2 2.37 Listen to the recording to check your answers. Repeat the words.

3 Rewrite the sentences in the past simple.

1 Every year, Michael and Violeta go to Poland for a holiday.
Last year, Michael and Violeta went to Poland for a holiday.
2 They go by plane from London.
3 They go to Warsaw.
4 They see their family and friends.
5 They drink Polish coffee.
6 They eat Polish food.
7 They have a good time.

4 2.38 Listen to the recording to check your answers. Repeat the sentences.

SPEAKING

1 Read the text about a person's holiday. Where was he?

I was on holiday last August.
I ate pizza and spaghetti.
I drank cappuccino.
I saw the Coliseum and the Sistine Chapel.
I went to …

2 2.39 Listen to the recording to check your answer.

3 Prepare a similar text about a real or imaginary holiday.

I was on holiday last …
I ate …
I drank …
I saw … and …

4 Work in pairs, A and B.

A: Tell B about your holiday.
B: Guess where A went on holiday.

5 Swap roles and repeat.

9B | Last days

Grammar: Past simple regular verbs (affirmative & negative)
Vocabulary: Music words; Songs
Reading: The Beatles' last concert

READING & VOCABULARY: music words

1 Do you know the British rock group the Beatles? Do you like them? Tell a partner.

2 The words in the box are all in the article. Check you understand the words. What do you think the article is about?

group studio roof crowd concert
legend play music

3 Read the article and check your answer to exercise 2.

It was a cold day in January, 1969. On Savile Row in London, Paul McCartney, John Lennon, George Harrison and Ringo Starr were in the Apple Music studios. It wasn't a good time for the Beatles. They didn't want to work together anymore. They hated being in the same room together.

They decided to do something different. Suddenly, the people in the street heard music. They didn't know what it was. They looked up and saw the Beatles on the roof of the building. Cars stopped in the middle of the street. People got out and listened. Secretaries in the offices on Savile Row opened their windows. Soon there was a large crowd. It was a free Beatles concert!

The Beatles stayed on the roof and played their music to the street. Then someone called the police. The police came and stopped the concert.

The 1969 rooftop concert became a legend in British pop music. After the concert, the Beatles didn't play together again in public. It was the end of the sixties. It was the end of the Beatles.

4 Read the article again. Complete the sentences with words from the box. There are two extra words.

police holiday friends concert
cars roof children

1 The Beatles' last ______ was in January.
2 The Beatles weren't good ______ at the time.
3 They played a concert on the ______.
4 People stopped their ______ and listened in the street.
5 The ______ stopped the concert.

GRAMMAR: past simple regular verbs (affirmative & negative)

For past simple regular verbs, add *-ed* to the verb.
The people ***listened*** *to the music.*
Negative: *didn't* + verb
They ***didn't*** *play together again.*
Negatives are the same for regular and irregular past simple verbs.

SEE LANGUAGE REFERENCE PAGE 94

1 Find all the examples of past simple verbs in the article in Reading & vocabulary exercise 3. Which are regular and which are irregular?

2 Complete the sentences. Put the verb in brackets into the past simple.

1 The Beatles ______ (*be*) in the studio.
2 They ______ (*not want*) to work together.
3 They ______ (*not like*) each other.
4 They ______ (*go*) to the rooftop and ______ (*start*) a concert.
5 People ______ (*look*) up.
6 Secretaries ______ (*open*) their windows.
7 Someone ______ (*call*) the police.
8 The concert ______ (*stop*).
9 The Beatles ______ (*not play*) together in public again.

Pronunciation: past simple regular verbs

1 2.40 Listen to the past simple regular verbs.

A		B	
work	worked	hate	hated
watch	watched	start	started
play	played	end	ended

2 2.40 Listen again and repeat. Which words have an extra syllable? A or B?

Speaking

1 Read about the history of the Beatles. Work in pairs. Make sentences. Tell the story of the Beatles.

A: *The Beatles were the most famous British rock group in history.*
B: *They were from Liverpool.*
A: *Their names were John, Paul, Ringo and George.*
B: *In 1957 John Lennon met Paul McCartney.*

English around you: songs

1 Many people learn English words from pop songs. Do you know these Beatles songs?

2 What are these song titles in your language?

3 Do you know other English words or phrases from songs? What are they?

THE HISTORY OF THE BEATLES

The most famous British rock group in history.

From:	Liverpool, UK
Names:	John, Paul, Ringo, George
1957	John Lennon meets Paul McCartney.
1961	The Beatles play their first concert.
1962	The Beatles release their first song, *Love Me Do*.
1964	The Beatles visit the United States. They are number 1 in the charts.
1968	The Beatles go to India.
1969	The Beatles play their last concert.
1970	The Beatles make their last album, *Let It Be*.
1980	John Lennon dies in New York.
2001	George Harrison dies.

9c | Independence day

Grammar: Prepositions of time (*in*, *on*, *at*)
Vocabulary: Months
Listening: Independence day holidays

Vocabulary: months

1 2.41 Listen and repeat the months of the year.

January	May	September
February	June	October
March	July	November
April	August	December

2 Work in pairs, A and B.

A: Say a month.
B: Say the month before and after.

A: March
B: February, April

3 What are your favourite months of the year? Tell a partner.

Listening

1 Look at the photos of two independence day holidays. What countries are these? Do you know these holidays?

2 2.42 Listen to two people talking about independence day holidays. Match the speakers to the photos.

Speaker 1 ______ Speaker 2 ______

3 2.42 Listen again. Who says it? Tick (✓) *Sandra* or *Charlie*.

	Sandra	Charlie
1 We have lots of holidays.		
2 I don't go to work.		
3 We got our independence from England.		
4 I usually have a big meal with my family in the evening.		
5 I always have a big barbecue with friends and family.		
6 It's a great day.		
7 There is always music and dancing.		

Functional language: the date

1 2.43 Listen and repeat.

A: What's the date today?
B: It's the fourth of July./It's July fourth.

2 2.44 With the date we use ordinal numbers. Listen and repeat the ordinal numbers.

first	sixth	eleventh
second	seventh	twelfth
third	eighth	twenty-first
fourth	ninth	twenty-second
fifth	tenth	twenty-third

3 2.45 Listen and answer the questions 1–6.

A

B

Pronunciation: /θ/ & /ð/

1 2.46 Listen and tick (✓) the word you hear.

1 four __ fourth __
2 six __ sixth __
3 sink __ think __
4 day __ they __
5 dare __ their __

2 2.47 Listen and repeat the sentences.

1 Today is Thursday the fourth.
2 The year is two thousand and thirteen.
3 Their mother is there.
4 I think it's her birthday.

Grammar: prepositions of time (*in, on, at*)

Use *in* with years and months.
***in** 1776, **in** July*
Use *on* with dates and days.
***on** March 5th, **on** Monday*
Use *at* with times.
***at** six o'clock, at 8pm*

See Language Reference page 94

1 Complete the sentences with *in* or *on*.

1 South Africa's Freedom Day is ____ April 27.
2 Morocco's Independence Day is ____ November.
3 India became independent from Britain ____ 1947.
4 Colombia's Independence Day is ____ July 20.
5 Finland became an independent country ____ December 6, 1917.
6 Brazil's Independence Day is ____ September.

2 Underline the correct preposition to complete the sentences.

1 My birthday is *in / on / at* June.
2 My English class finishes *in / on / at* eight o'clock.
3 I never work *in / on / at* Sunday.
4 I was born *in / on / at* 1965.
5 The next holiday is *in / on / at* May 1st.

3 Make the sentences in exercise 2 true for you.

Speaking

1 Make questions from the prompts.

1 What / be / an important date in your country? be / it / an independence day?
2 you / like / this day? Why or why not?
3 What / you / usually do / on this day?
4 What / be / your favourite day of the year?

2 Work in pairs. Interview your partner with the questions in exercise 1.

Useful language

Our national holiday is on …
We usually have a picnic/go to a party/go on a parade/visit friends or family.
We work/don't work on this day.

9D | Review

Vocabulary

1 Which is correct, a or b?

	a)	b)
1	a) two millions	b) two million
2	a) a hundred and ten	b) hundred ten
3	a) two thousand four hundred	b) two thousand and four hundred
4	a) fifty thousands	b) fifty thousand

2 Work in pairs, A and B.

A: Write five big numbers. Don't show B. Read your numbers to B.
B: Write the numbers A says. Compare your numbers with the original. Were you right?

3 Swap roles and repeat.

Listening

1 2.48 Listen and complete the facts with a number.

A Hard Day's Night – The Beatles by numbers!

Number of songs: (1) ____
Number of singles: (2) ____
Number of CDs: (3) ____
Number of Beatles live concerts: (4) ____
Number of copies of *1* sold in first month: more than (5) ____

2 Check your answers in audioscript 2.48 on page 124. Say the numbers out loud.

Grammar

1 Complete the text with the past simple of the verbs in brackets.

MY FIRST ROCK CONCERT

I (1) ____ (*go*) to my first rock concert last August. I (2) ____ (*be*) in Berlin with my girlfriend. She (3) ____ (*want*) to see a new German group. We (4) ____ (*get*) tickets in the city centre. The concert (5) ____ (*start*) at ten o'clock. We (6) ____ (*have*) dinner first, and we (7) ____ (*arrive*) at the concert at nine thirty. It (8) ____ (*be*) in a small club. The group (9) ____ (*play*) for two hours. It (10) ____ (*be*) very noisy. My girlfriend (11) ____ (*love*) the concert, but I (12) ____ (*not like*) it. I don't remember the name of the group.

2 2.49 Listen to the sentences. Underline *past* or *present* for the sentences.

1 *past / present*
2 *past / present*
3 *past / present*
4 *past / present*
5 *past / present*

3 2.49 Listen again and write the sentences.

Reading & vocabulary

1 Read about the origin of the English names for the days. Complete the text with the names of days.

File Edit View Favourites Tools Help Links

ROME

From Roman times

The origins of the English names for the days come from old English and have origins in Ancient Rome and Germanic languages. Can you guess the answer to the questions below?

Which day is named after …
the sun? (1) ______
Thor, the Norse god of thunder? (2) ______
the moon? (3) ______
the planet Saturn? (4) ______

Functional language

1 Work in pairs, A and B.

A: Say one of the dates in the box.
B: Say why the date is important.

A: January 26th.
B: That's Burns Night.

IMPORTANT DATES

GREAT BRITAIN

May Day	01/05
New Year's Day	01/01
Guy Fawkes Day	05/11
Remembrance Day	11/11
Boxing Day	26/12
Burns Night (Scotland)	26/01

2 Swap roles and repeat.

Speaking

1 Think of two important dates in the year and write them on a piece of paper.

2 For each date, think of …

- something you always do.
- something you never do.
- something you sometimes do.

3 Work in pairs. Tell your partner about your important dates.

Self-assessment (✓)

- ☐ I can understand and say large numbers.
- ☐ I can describe a holiday I had in simple language.
- ☐ I can say the date.

10A | Good weekend!

Grammar: Past simple questions (1)
Vocabulary: Weekend activities
Listening: Dialogue about the weekend

VOCABULARY: weekend activities

1 Match the weekend activities 1–4 to the photos A–C. One activity is not needed.

1 make a meal
2 clean the house
3 go away
4 do the shopping

2 Complete the sentences with words from the box.

do	make	go	clean

At the weekend I usually …

1 _____ away.
out.

2 _____ a big breakfast.
dinner for my family.

3 _____ the house.
the car.

4 _____ the shopping.
nothing.

3 2.50 Listen to the recording to check your answers. Repeat the phrases.

4 Complete the sentences so that they are true for you. Use the phrases from exercise 1.

At the weekend I usually …
I never …
I sometimes …

5 Work in pairs. Compare your answers to exercise 4.

LISTENING

1 2.51 Listen to a man and woman talking about their weekends. Tick (✓) the phrases you hear.

1 did nothing much __
2 went to the disco __
3 did the shopping __
4 saw a film __
5 saw the football match __
6 went away __
7 went to Rome __

2 2.51 Listen again and choose the correct answer, a, b or c.

1 The man cleaned …
a) his car.
b) his house.
c) his room.

2 The man …
a) did the shopping and watched TV.
b) did the shopping but didn't watch TV.
c) watched TV but didn't do the shopping.

3 The woman went …
a) to France.
b) to Italy.
c) to England.

4 The woman went away …
a) with her family.
b) with a man.
c) with a woman.

5 The woman had …
a) a boring weekend.
b) an awful weekend.
c) a good weekend.

PRONUNCIATION: diphthongs

1 2.52 Listen to the words and sounds.

/aɪ/	/eɪ/	/aʊ/	/əʊ/
time	make	out	go

2 Put the words from the box in the correct column in exercise 1.

break house wife photo train white
play no nice brown thousand don't

3 2.53 Listen to the recording to check your answers. Say the words.

GRAMMAR: past simple questions (1)

For questions in the past simple use the auxiliary *did*.
did + subject + infinitive
Did *you go out?* ***Did*** *she have a good time?*
Short answers
Yes, I did. No, I didn't. Yes, she did. No, she didn't.
With *wh*- questions, put the question word in front of *did*.
Where *did you go?*

SEE LANGUAGE REFERENCE PAGE 94

1 2.54 Listen to the questions. Answer, *Yes, I did* or *No, I didn't*.

2 Change the sentences to questions.

1 I went out after work.
Did you go out after work?
2 I watched TV.
3 I used the internet.
4 I went out.
5 I did my English homework.

3 Make questions from the prompts.

1 What time / you / start work?
What time did you start work?
2 What time / you / finish work?
3 How / you / get home?
4 Where / you / go after work?
5 What / you / have / for dinner?

4 Work in pairs, A and B.

A: Ask B about last night. Use the questions in exercise 2. Answer B's questions.
B: Ask A about yesterday. Use the questions in exercise 3. Answer A's questions.

SPEAKING

1 Work in pairs, A and B. Have a dialogue about the weekend. Use the diagram below and the expressions in the Useful language box to help you.

A: Ask B, *How was your weekend?*
B: Answer A.
A: Ask, *What did you do?*
B: Tell A two things you did.
A: Respond.
B: Ask A, *What did you do at the weekend?*
A: Tell B one or two things you did.
B: Respond.

2 Now work with another student and repeat the dialogue.

Useful language

Responses
Really?
That's great.
That sounds nice.
That sounds awful.
Oh no.

10B | Good question!

Grammar: Past simple questions (2)
Functional language: Guessing
Reading: Quizzes in Britain

Reading

1 Look at the photos of a quiz night. What do you think people do at these events, 1, 2 or 3?

1 Have a song and dance competition.
2 Ask and answer questions.
3 Talk about problems in the neighbourhood.

2 Read the text and check your answer to exercise 1.

QUIZ NIGHT

A quiz night (also called a 'trivia night') is a popular game in Britain. People play the game in teams. A person (the quizmaster) reads out a question and the teams write their answers on a piece of paper. At the end of the quiz, the team with the most correct answers wins a prize. There are hundreds of thousands of quiz nights every week in Britain.

3 Are quiz games popular in your country? Why or why not?

Functional language: guessing

1 2.55 Listen to two people at a quiz. Complete the dialogue with words from the box.

sure think maybe

Man: I (1) ______ it's Kiev.
Woman: (2) ______ it's Riga.
Man: No, I'm (3) ______ it's Kiev.

2 Work in pairs. What do these phrases mean in your language?

3 2.55 Listen again and repeat.

Listening

1 Work in teams of three or four. You are going to do a quiz. Read the quiz sheet below.

2 2.56 Listen to the questions and choose the correct answer, a, b or c.

QUIZ SHEET

HISTORY

1 a) 20 July 1969.
b) 1 June 1969.
c) 1 July 1991.

SPORTS

2 a) Paris.
b) Athens.
c) New York.

SCIENCE AND NATURE

3 a) Asia.
b) Latin America.
c) Europe.

FILM

4 a) Sean Connery.
b) Daniel Craig.
c) Roger Moore.

MUSIC

5 a) 1972.
b) 1970.
c) 1971.

3 2.56 Listen again and check your answers with the others on your team. Then listen to the teacher give the correct answers.

GRAMMAR: past simple questions (2)

Remember the word order for questions in the past simple.

Questions with verb *to be*

(question word) + *was/were* + subject

*Where **was he** born?*

***Were you** at the quiz night?*

Questions with other verbs

(question word) + *did* + subject + verb

***Did you win** a prize?*

***What did you win**?*

For *yes/no* questions, remember the short answer form.

Yes, I was.

Yes, I did.

No, I wasn't.

No, I didn't.

SEE LANGUAGE REFERENCE PAGE 94

1 Rearrange the words to make the questions from the quiz.

1 Neil Armstrong walk When on the did moon ?
2 Where the first were modern Olympic Games ?
3 potatoes come from Where originally did ?
4 James Bond Who first was the ?
5 the Beatles break up When did ?

2 Make questions for another category using key words.

1 When / the US / get / its independence from England?
2 What sport / Greg LeMond and Marco Pantani / do?
3 Where / the group Abba / come from?
4 Who / be / the author of *Oliver Twist*?
5 What year / the film *Titanic* / win eleven Oscars™?
6 Where / Elvis Presley / come from?

3 Match the questions 1–6 in exercise 2 to the answers a–f.

a Cycling.
b Charles Dickens.
c Mississippi, US.
d 1776.
e Sweden.
f 1997.

PRONUNCIATION: connected speech (2)

1 2.57 Listen to the sentences. How many words do you hear (contractions = two words)?

2 Look at audioscript 2.57 on page 124 and check your answers. Say the phrases quickly.

SPEAKING

1 Work in teams. Prepare five questions for a quiz. Use the phrases in the box to help you.

When did …? Who was …?
Where was …? Where did … come from?
Who was the author of …?

2 Work with another group. Take turns. Ask your questions. Answer the other group's questions.

10c | Good deal

Vocabulary: Money & prices; Clothes labels
Functional language: In a shop
Reading: *Night markets – the place for a good deal*

Speaking & reading

1 Work in pairs. Do the shopping questionnaire.

SHOPPING QUESTIONNAIRE

1. Do you like shopping?
2. How often do you go shopping?
3. Did you go shopping last weekend?
4. What did you buy?
5. What are the best places to go shopping in your town?

2 Look at the photos and read the article. What do you think *a good deal* means, 1, 2 or 3?

1 something cheap
2 something expensive
3 something good quality

3 Read the article again and answer the questions.

1 When are night markets open?
2 Where are night markets popular?
3 What do people buy at night markets?
4 What are the prices?

4 Work in pairs. Do you know any night markets? Would you like to shop at a night market? Why or why not?

Night markets – the place for a good deal

A night market is a market that is open only at night. Many countries in Asia, for example Taiwan, Thailand, China, Malaysia and Indonesia have a tradition of night markets. In some places night markets are popular because it is very hot during the day (for example in Bangkok, Thailand). Night markets are popular places to buy toys, clothes, films and souvenirs. They often open after 6pm and don't close before midnight. The prices are often very cheap. Night markets are good places to find a good deal.

Vocabulary: money & prices

1 Match the words 1–5 to the prices A–E.

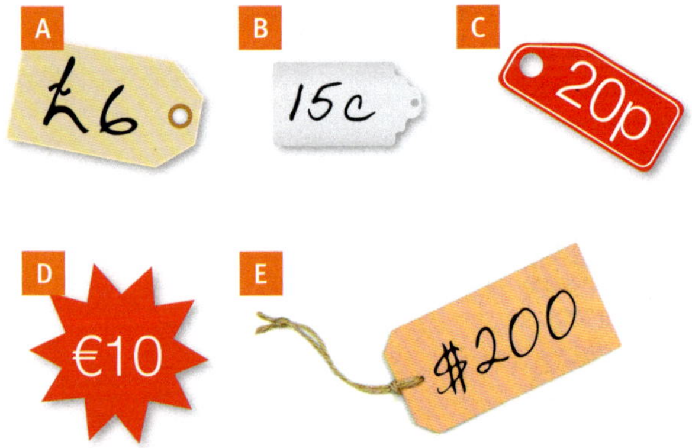

1 ten euros
2 fifteen cents
3 six pounds
4 twenty pence (twenty p)
5 two hundred dollars

2 2.58 Listen to the recording to check your answers.

3 2.59 Listen and repeat.

1 How much is it?
It's $6.99.
It's six ninety-nine. It's six dollars and ninety-nine cents.
2 How much is it?
It's €3.50.
It's three fifty. It's three euros and fifty cents.
3 How much is it?
It's £25.59.
It's twenty-five fifty-nine. It's twenty-five pounds and fifty-nine p.

4 Work in pairs, A and B. Look at page 115. Practise asking for prices.

LISTENING

1 2.60 Listen and match the dialogues 1–4 to the pictures A–D.

A

1 ______

B

2 ______

C

3 ______

D

4 ______

2 2.60 Listen again. Complete the sentences with words and phrases from the box.

where	help	bag	credit card	excuse
thanks	six hundred			

1
A: Hello, can I ______ you?
B: I'm just looking, ______.

2
A: ______ me?
B: Yes?
A: ______ are the changing rooms?

3
A: How much is this?
B: It's ______ pounds.
C: I love it.
A: Can I pay by ______?

4
A: Would you like a ______ for that?
B: Yes, please.

FUNCTIONAL LANGUAGE: in a shop

1 Who says it? Mark the sentences *C* for the customer and *SA* for the shop assistant.

1 Can I help you? ______
2 I'm just looking, thanks. ______
3 Where are the changing rooms? ______
4 How much is this? ______
5 It's 600 pounds. ______
6 Can I pay by credit card? ______

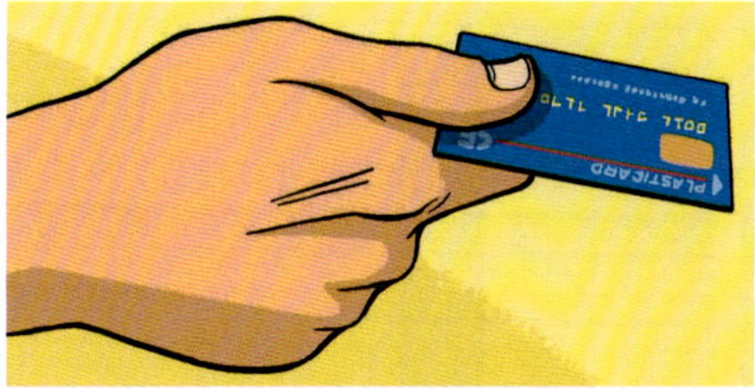

2 Work in pairs. Look at audioscript 2.60 on page 125 and check your answers. Practise the dialogues.

SPEAKING

1 Work in pairs, A and B.

A: Turn to page 119.
B: Turn to page 116.

Roleplay a shopping dialogue.

ENGLISH AROUND YOU: clothes labels

1 Read the examples of English on labels. What are these words in your language?

2 Do you know any English words from labels or British or American shop names? What are they?

10D | Review

Vocabulary & speaking

1 Complete the words and expressions in the diagram.

What do the British do at weekends?

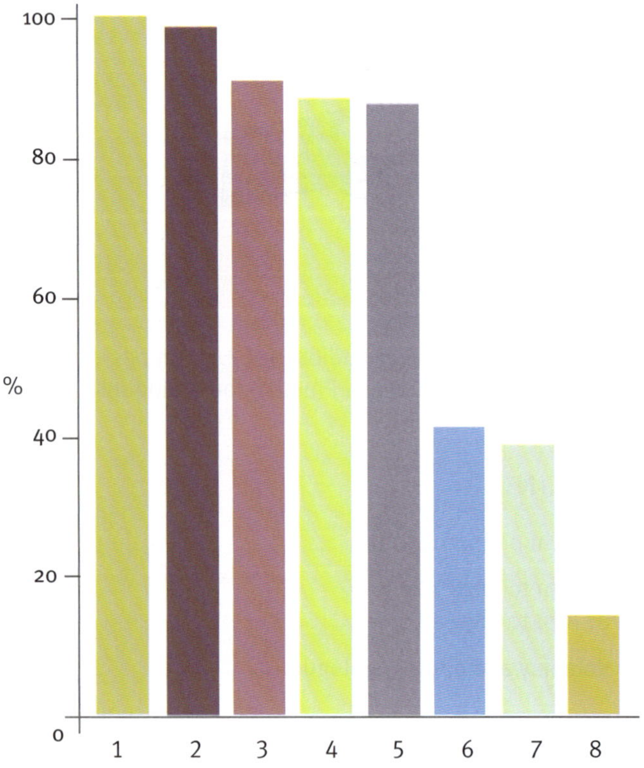

- (1) S_____p 100%
- (2) Eat and d_____k 98%
- (3) C_____n the house 91%
- (4) G_____ out or g_____ away 88%
- (5) W_____h TV 87%
- (6) R_____d a book or newspaper 42%
- (7) W_____rk 39%
- (8) D_____ sport 15%

2 Do you think these statistics are similar for your country? Make a list with a partner of popular weekend activities.

3 Work with another pair. Explain your lists.

Reading

1 Read the article about weekends. Match the texts 1–3 to the people A–C.

What did you do this weekend?

_____
1
This weekend wasn't very interesting. I played video games in my room. I talked on the phone to my friends. My mum and dad did nothing at the weekend, they only watched television on Sunday night.

_____
2
On Saturday I did the shopping for the family. I made lunch for my son, he was in his room. On Saturday afternoon I cleaned the house. On Sunday I made lunch and dinner for the family. On Sunday night I watched my favourite television show with my husband. I was very tired.

_____
3
I worked on the computer at home on Saturday morning. On Saturday afternoon I cleaned the car. I did nothing on Sunday, it's my rest day. I had lunch and dinner with my family and watched television with my wife in the evening.

2 Read the article again and complete the sentences with The mother (*M*), The father (*F*) or The son (*S*).

1 _____ cleaned the house.
2 _____ cleaned the car.
3 _____ made lunch and dinner on Sunday.
4 _____ played video games.
5 _____ did nothing on Sunday.

3 Think of a typical weekend in your family. What do people do? Tell a partner.

Grammar

1 Decide if the questions are correct or incorrect. Correct the false sentences.

1 Did you away last August?
2 What did you have for breakfast?
3 How you come to class today?
4 What time you did wake up this morning?
5 Did you watch TV last night?

2 Work in pairs. Ask and answer the questions in exercise 1.

Vocabulary

1 2.61 Listen and tick (✓) the price you hear.

1	a) $16.15 __	b) $16.50 __
2	a) €200 __	b) €2,000 __
3	a) 80p __	b) 18p __
4	a) £1.99 __	b) £199.00 __

2 Say the prices.

Functional language

1 Rearrange the words to make sentences or questions.

☐ 1 book this How much is ?
☐ 2 card credit I Can pay by ?
☐ 3 25 It's euros .
☐ 4 of Yes, course .
☐ 5 I Can you help ?

2 The sentences in exercise 1 are part of a dialogue in a shop. Put the sentences in the correct order.

3 2.62 Listen to the recording to check your answers.

Speaking

1 Look at the photos of different objects on sale in a night market. Can you guess what the objects are? Choose from the words below. There is one extra word you do not need.

a phrase book   jewellery   a phone
a computer   a bag   an umbrella
sunglasses   make up   a souvenir

2 Look at page 117 to check your answers.

Useful language

I'm sure it's a/they're …
Maybe they are/it is …
I think it's a/they're …

Self-assessment (✓)

☐ I can say what I did last weekend.
☐ I can use language to make guesses.
☐ I can say prices.
☐ I can ask for prices and things in a shop.

9 & 10 Language reference

Grammar
Past simple

There are two kinds of past simple verbs in English.
Regular verbs: these verbs take *-ed* for the past simple.

walk – walked
stop – stopped
start – started

Irregular verbs: these verbs change form in the past simple.

eat – ate
go – went
make – made
see – saw
have – had

Many common verbs are irregular in the past simple. There is a list of irregular verbs on page 127.

affirmative		
I You He/She/It We They	went	to India.

For negatives, use the auxiliary *did* and *not (didn't)* and the infinitive.

negative			
I You He/She/It We They	didn't	go	to India.

For questions, use the auxiliary *did*. Put the auxiliary before the subject and the infinitive after the subject.

question			
Did	I you he/she/it we they	go	to India?

short answer		
Yes,	I you he/she/it we they	did.
No,		didn't.

Prepositions of time (*in*, *on*, *at*)

Use *in* with months, years.
***in** 2001, **in** July*

Use *on* with dates, days.
***on** April 4th, **on** Monday*

Use *at* with times.
***at** six o'clock*
Note: ***at** the weekend, **at** night*

Functional language

Guessing

I think it's Kiev.
Maybe it's Riga.
No, I'm sure it's Kiev.

In a shop

Can I help you?
It's 600 pounds.
I'm just looking, thanks.
Where are the changing rooms?
How much is this?
Can I pay by credit card?

The date

What's the date today?
It's the (fourth of July).
It's (July fourth).

Word list

Big numbers

hundred **	/ˈhʌndrəd/
thousand **	/ˈθaʊz(ə)nd/
million **	/ˈmɪljən/
billion **	/ˈbɪljən/

Months

January *n* ***	/ˈdʒænjuəri/
February *n* ***	/ˈfebruəri/
March *n* ***	/mɑː(r)tʃ/
April *n* ***	/ˈeɪprəl/
May *n* ***	/meɪ/
June *n* ***	/dʒuːn/
July *n* ***	/dʒʊˈlaɪ/
August *n* ***	/ˈɔːgəst/
September *n* ***	/sepˈtembə(r)/
October *n* ***	/ɒkˈtəʊbə(r)/
November *n* ***	/nəʊˈvembə(r)/
December *n* ***	/dɪˈsembə(r)/

Weekend activities

clean *v* ***	/kliːn/
do *v* ***	/duː/
go away *v*	/ˌgəʊ əˈweɪ/
go out *v*	/ˌgəʊ ˈaʊt/
make *v* ***	/meɪk/

Money & prices

buy *v* ***	/baɪ/
cent *n*	/sent/
cheap *adj* ***	/tʃiːp/
dollar *n* **	/ˈdɒlə(r)/
euro *n* *	/ˈjʊərəʊ/
expensive *adj* ***	/ɪkˈspensɪv/
pence *n*	/pens/
pound *n* ***	/paʊnd/
shopping *n* ***	/ˈʃɒpɪŋ/

Music words

album *n* **	/ˈælbəm/
charts *n* **	/tʃɑː(r)ts/
concert *n* **	/ˈkɒnsə(r)t/
crowd *n* ***	/kraʊd/
group *n* ***	/gruːp/
legend *n*	/ˈledʒ(ə)nd/
studio *n* ***	/ˈstjuːdiəʊ/

Other words & phrases

bag *n* ***	/ˌbæg/
barbeque *n* *	/ˈbɑː(r)bɪˌkjuː/
birthday *n* **	/ˈbɜː(r)θdeɪ/
building *n* ***	/ˈbɪldɪŋ/
call *v* ***	/kɔːl/
clothes *n* ***	/kləʊðz/
cold adj ***	/kəʊld/
crowded *adj* *	/ˈkraʊdɪd/
deal *n* ***	/diːl/
dish *n* **	/dɪʃ/
find *v* ***	/faɪnd/
free *adj* ***	/friː/
hate *v* ***	/heɪt/
hear *v* ***	/hɪə(r)/
independence *n* ***	/ˌɪndɪˈpendəns/
last *adj* ***	/lɑːst/
market *n* *	/ˈmɑː(r)kɪt/
noisy *adj* *	/ˈnɔɪzi/
piece of paper	/ˌpiːs əv ˈpeɪpə(r)/
popular *adj* ***	/ˈpɒpjʊlə(r)/
quiz *n* *	/kwɪz/
roof *n* ***	/ruːf/
say	/seɪ/
souvenir *n* *	/ˌsuːvəˈnɪə(r)/
stay *v* ***	/steɪ/
stop *n* ***	/stɒp/
together *adv* ***	/təˈgeðə(r)/
tradition *n* ***	/trəˈdɪʃ(ə)n/
trivia *n*	/ˈtrɪviə/
watch *v* ***	/wɒtʃ/
world *n* ***	/wɜː(r)ld/

11A | Special people

Grammar: *Can/can't*
Vocabulary: Action verbs
Reading: *People look at us*

Vocabulary: action verbs

1 2.63 Listen and match the verbs 1–8 to the pictures A–H.

A

B

C

D

E

F

G

H

1 type
2 *walk*
3 sing
4 swim
5 dance
6 *drive*
7 run
8 play guitar

2 Cover the words. Look at the pictures and say the verbs.

Reading

1 Read the article about different people on page 97. What is it about?

2 Read the article again and complete the sentences *N* for Nathan, *J* for Janice and *I* for Isaac.

1 _____ uses a computer at work.
2 _____ knows many different languages.
3 _____ does sports.
4 _____ works with the internet.
5 _____ won a medal last year.
6 _____ works in the US.

3 Each of the people in the article has a disability. Turn to page 118 to find out more.

4 Work in pairs. Do you know someone who has a disability? Tell your partner about them.

Grammar: *can/can't*

Use *can* + verb to talk about ability.
*I **can** act.*
Can is the same form for all subjects.
I/you/he/she/it/we/they ***can***
The negative of *can* is *can't*.

Questions
Can + subject + verb + …?
***Can** you dance?*

Short answer
*Yes, I **can**.* *No, I **can't**.*

See Language Reference page 112

1 Correct the four mistakes with *can* in the text.

Our son Charles was born with cerebral palsy. Charles don't can walk and he doesn't can run with the other children. But he can do lots of other things. He cans read, he can write his name and he can to use a computer. That's not bad for a four-year-old.

2 2.64 Listen to check your answers.

PEOPLE LOOK AT US
and always see what we can't do.

They don't think about what we can do.

The artist

My name's Nathan. I work for a big company. I'm a graphic artist. I make websites. I can type fast – 114 words a minute!

The actor

I'm Janice. I'm an actor. I can act, I can sing and I can dance. I speak English, French and Spanish and I work on Broadway, New York.

The athlete

My name's Isaac and I'm an athlete. I can swim and play tennis. Last year, I was in a national tennis competition. I won.

PRONUNCIATION: *can/can't*

1 2.65 Listen to the pronunciation of *can* in these sentences.

I <u>can</u> drive.	I <u>can't</u> drive.	<u>Can</u> you drive?
/kən/	/kaːnt/	/kæn/

2 2.66 Listen and write the sentences you hear. Practise saying the sentences.

SPEAKING

1 What can you do in English? Tick (✓) the phrases in the box that are true for you.

The English Challenge!

- count to 20 ☐
- spell your name ☐
- say your email address ☐
- say your phone number ☐
- introduce yourself ☐
- say what you did on Saturday ☐
- tell the time ☐
- say the date ☐
- describe the classroom ☐

2 2.67 Read and listen to the example.

A: Can you spell your name in English?
B: Yes, I can.
A: Show me.
B: M-I-C-H-A-E-L.

3 Work in pairs, A and B. Play *The English Challenge!* game.

A: Can you … in English?
B: Yes, I can./No, I can't.
A: Show me.

11B | Special event

Grammar: Present continuous
Vocabulary: International organizations
Listening: At a concert

Speaking

1 Work in pairs. Look at the photos at the bottom of the page and answer the questions.

1 What can you see?
2 Where are the people?
3 Would you like to be there? Why or why not?

Listening

1 2.68 Listen to the telephone dialogues 1–4 at this event. Which dialogue ...

a talks about food? ____
b talks about work? ____
c talks about clothes? ____
d is in the car? ____

2 2.68 Listen again and choose the correct phrase, a or b, to complete the sentences.

1 Speaker 1 is ...
a) in front of the gates.
b) at the front gates.

2 Speaker 2 is getting something ...
a) to eat.
b) to drink.

3 Speaker 3 is wearing ...
a) a blue jacket.
b) a red jacket.

4 Speaker 4 is having ...
a) a good time.
b) a bad time.

Grammar: present continuous

Use the present continuous to talk about things happening now.
subject + *to be* + verb + *-ing*
*I **am** driv**ing**.*
Question
(question word) + *to be* + subject + verb + *-ing*
*What **are** you do**ing**?*
***Is** it rain**ing**?*
Negative
subject + *to be* + *not* (*n't*) + verb + *-ing*
*I'm **not** work**ing**.*

See Language Reference page 112

1 2.69 Listen to the sounds and make a sentence with one of the verbs from the box. Use the present continuous.

have a shower   talk on the phone
drive   play guitar   type

1 He ...   2 They ...   3 She ...   4 They ...   5 She ...

2 Complete the dialogue with the present continuous form of the verbs in brackets.

A: Hello?
B: Hello, darling, it's your mother. How are you?
A: Fine, thanks.
B: What ____ you ____ (*do*)? What's that noise?
A: I'm at a concert. The band ____ (*play*). People ____ (*dance*) and ... it's a bit crazy.
B: Oh, that sounds nice. When does the concert finish?
A: What?
B: Darling, you ____ (*not listen*).
A: I ____ (*listen*), Mum, but I can't hear you! John and Liz ____ (*talk*) at the same time ... Quiet, I ____ (*use*) the phone!
B: Hello? Hello? Oh dear, his phone ____ (*not work*) now.

3 2.70 Listen to the recording to check your answers.

Pronunciation: /ŋ/

1 2.71 Listen and repeat the sound and words.

/ŋ/ havi<u>ng</u> thi<u>ng</u> eati<u>ng</u>

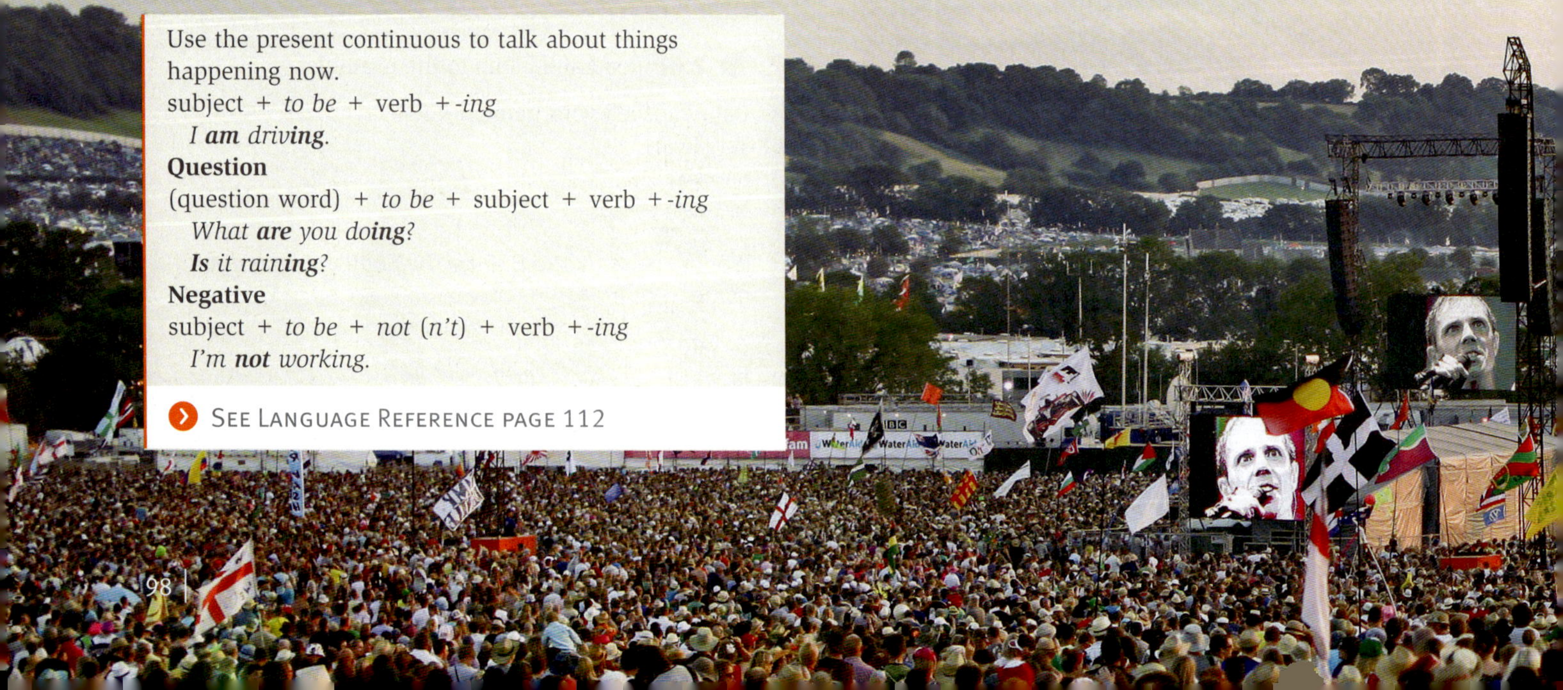

2 Underline the words with the /ŋ/ sound in the sentences. Practise saying the sentences.

1 I'm going to the bank.
2 She's speaking French.
3 I can't think.
4 Is English a difficult language?

Speaking

1 2.72 Read and listen to the dialogue. Match it to one of the pictures A–D.

A: Hi, how are you?
B: I'm fine.
A: Can you talk right now?
B: Yes, I can.
A: What are you doing?
B: I'm at home. I'm watching TV.

A

B

C

D

2 Work in pairs. Choose a different picture and make a similar dialogue.

3 Roleplay your dialogue.

English around you: international organizations

1 2.73 Glastonbury Festival is famous for its music, but also for social causes. Listen to the names of some well-known non-governmental organizations.

FAIRTRADE FOUNDATION
ICRC
GREENPEACE
Save the Children

2 Which organizations do you know? What are they in your language?

3 Do you know any other English names for international organizations? What are they?

11c | Special paintings

Functional language: Talking about a painting
Reading: *Special paintings*
Listening: Dialogues about paintings

SPEAKING & READING

1 Work in pairs. Look at the paintings and discuss the questions.

1 Do you know these paintings?
2 What do you think of them?

2 Read the article. What is the connection between the article and the paintings?

Special paintings

In 2005, the National Gallery of London and the BBC had a competition to find Britain's favourite painting. More than 118,000 people voted. The competition made people talk and think more about art. Here are some of the favourite paintings.

3 Read the article again and answer the questions.

1 What was the competition about?
2 When was the competition?
3 Why did the National Gallery and the BBC organize the competition?
4 How many people voted?

4 Work in pairs. Ask and answer the questions.

1 Would you like to vote in an art competition?
2 Which painting would you like to win?
3 Is art popular in your country?
4 What artists do you like?

Sunflowers by Vincent Van Gogh 1888

A Bar at the Folies-Bergère by Edouard Manet 1882

The Fighting Temeraire by JMW Turner 1839

Listening

1 2.74 Listen to people talking about the paintings on page 100. Put the paintings in the order you hear them.

2 2.74 Listen again and decide if the sentences are true (T) or false (F). Correct the false sentences.

1 This painting is not very popular.
2 Van Gogh painted this while he was in France.
3 The woman is in Paris.
4 Maybe the woman is sad.
5 *The Temeraire* is a famous boat.
6 *The Temeraire* is the small boat.

Functional language: talking about a painting

1 Match the sentences 1–3 to the paintings A–C on page 100.

1 In this painting I can see a woman at a bar.
2 The flowers are yellow.
3 There are two boats on the river.

2 2.75 Listen and repeat the sentences.

3 Make other sentences about the paintings on page 100.

Language note

Use the present continuous to talk about paintings.
The small boat ***is pulling*** *the big boat.*
The men ***are drinking****.*

Speaking

1 Look at another favourite painting. Make notes about what you see. Use the questions in the box to help you.

What can you see? Where are they?
What are they doing?
What are they thinking about?

2 Work in pairs. Talk about the painting.

Automat by Edward Hopper 1927

11D | Review

Listening

1 2.76 Listen to a job interview. What is the problem?

2 2.76 Listen again and tick (✓) the correct sentences, a or b.

1 a) The man can sing. __
  b) The man can't sing. __
2 a) The man can't dance. __
  b) The man can dance. __
3 a) The man wants a job at tourist information. __
  b) The man wants a job as a television actor. __
4 a) The man is in room 3. __
  b) The man is in room 4. __

Grammar & vocabulary

1 Make sentences about the people in Listening exercise 1 in the present continuous affirmative or negative.

1 The man / sit.
The man is sitting.
2 He / stand.
He isn't standing.
3 The woman / listen to music.
4 They / talk.
5 The woman / look for a job.
6 The man / look for a job.
7 They / have lunch.
8 They / have a job interview.

2 Look at the pictures. Complete the sentences with *can/can't* and a verb from the box. There is one extra verb.

run	eat	play	see	dance	drive

1 Sorry, I ______.

2 She ______ fast.

3 He ______ tonight.

4 I ______ this guitar.

5 ______ you ______ me?

3 Test your memory. Cover the sentences. Look at the pictures and say the sentences.

4 Work in pairs. Complete the sentences so that they are true for you.

We can … *We can't …*
I can …, but my partner can't.

Functional language

1 Rearrange the words to make sentences.

1 Van Gogh think I a it's painting .
2 this photo in are four There men .
3 I France think in it's .
4 men are The sleeping .
5 I see can café this painting In a .
6 Maybe New York in this is .

2 Match the sentences 1–6 in exercise 1 to a picture, A or B. Say the sentences.

3 What do you think? Do you like these pictures? Ask and answer with a partner.

A

Speaking

1 Work in pairs, A and B.

A: Turn to page 114.
B: Turn to page 119.

Find four differences in your pictures.

Self-assessment (✓)

☐ I can talk about what I am doing at the moment.
☐ I can describe a picture.
☐ I can talk about ability.

B

12A The phone

Vocabulary: Telephoning
Functional language: Telephone English
Reading: *Me and my mobile*

Speaking & reading

1 Work in pairs. Complete the sentences with a word or words so that they are true for you. Then compare with a partner.

1 I have *one* / *more than one* mobile phone/s.
2 I *have* / *don't have* a smartphone.
3 I *know* / *don't know* everything my phone can do.
4 I *use* / *don't use* my phone to take photos.
5 I *use* / *don't use* my phone to go on the internet.
6 I *like* / *don't like* mobile phones.

2 Read the article about people and their mobile phones.

1 Who likes mobile phones?
2 Who doesn't like mobile phones?

ME AND MY MOBILE

This is my mobile phone. It has a camera, an mp3 player and a little television. It's very small. I love it. It's my fourth or fifth mobile phone. I change phones very often and I always have the new model.
Sara, Spain

I have a mobile phone, but I don't use it often. I don't like them very much. I always forget to turn it off. And when I turn it off, I forget to turn it on again. The other problem is: when I want my mobile phone, I can't find it!
Clark, UK

My husband and I bought a mobile phone for our daughter. We thought it was a good idea. We could call her if we didn't know where she was. But now she uses it all the time to talk to friends and send messages. It's a lot of money and who pays? Her parents! We don't think it's a good idea now.
Pavla, Czech Republic

3 Read the article again and decide if the sentences are true (T) or false (F). Correct the false sentences.

1 Sara's phone is very old.
2 Sara changes phones often.
3 Clark forgets to turn on his mobile phone.
4 Clark doesn't use his mobile phone very much.
5 Pavla's daughter has a mobile phone.
6 Pavla doesn't pay for the mobile phone.

4 Are you similar to Sara, Clark or Pavla?

Vocabulary: telephoning

1 Complete the sentences with words from the box.

turn on	turn off	call	send

1 Please ______ your mobile phones in the cinema.
2 Can you ______ a text message with the information, please?
3 After class I always ______ my phone and listen to the messages.
4 Sorry I didn't ______ you last night. I didn't have your phone number with me.

2 2.77 Listen to check your answers. Repeat the sentences.

Listening

1 Look at the picture of Clark. Answer the questions.

1 What is Clark doing?
2 Why is he angry?

2 2.78 Listen and put the phone calls in the correct order.

- ☐ Clark calls Sara's work.
- ☐ Clark calls the wrong number.
- ☐ Clark calls Sara's home.

3 2.78 Listen again and <u>underline</u> the correct word.

1 Clark *can / can't* use the mobile phone inside the building.
2 Clark calls the *right / wrong* phone number.
3 Sara *is / isn't* at work today.
4 *Clark / Sara* is at the library, but *Clark / Sara* is at home.

Pronunciation & functional language

Intonation (4) (telephone English)

1 2.79 Read and listen to the phrases.

Hello, this is Sandra.
Hello, it's Sandra.

Is that Mike?
Can I speak to Mike?
Is Mike there?

I'm sorry, Mike isn't here.
Can I take a message?
Would you like to call back?

2 2.80 Listen to four of the phone phrases in exercise 1 again. Repeat the phrases and copy the intonation.

3 Cross out the incorrect option, a, b or c, for each dialogue.

Hello.	a) Hello, this is Clark. b) Hello, I'm Clark. c) Hello, it's Clark.
Hello, Clark.	a) Is that Sara? b) Are you Sara? c) Sara?
No, it's Paula.	a) I can speak to Sara? b) Can I speak to Sara? c) Is Sara there?
Just a minute. I'm sorry, Sara's not here.	a) Please tell her I called. b) Please say her I called. c) Please tell her Clark called.

4 Work in pairs. Make dialogues with the phrases. Pay attention to intonation.

Speaking

1 2.81 Read and listen to the dialogue. Match it to one of the pictures A–C.

A

B

C

Man: Hello.
Woman: Hello, is that George?
Man: No, it's Randall.
Woman: Is George there, please?
Man: Yes, he is. Just a minute.
Woman: Thank you.
George: Hello?
Woman: George! When ARE you coming home? Dinner was ready at eight o'clock!
George: Oh. Sorry. I'm in a meeting, but I'm coming home now.
Woman: Hmph!

2 Choose another picture and prepare a similar dialogue.

12B The airport

Grammar: *Going to* (1) future plans
Vocabulary: At the airport
Listening: At the airport

Speaking

1 Look at the picture of the airport terminal. Work in pairs, A and B.

A: Describe something you see.
B: Point to the part of the picture A describes.

A: He's talking on the phone.
B: Here.
A: Right.

2 Swap roles and repeat.

Listening

1 2.82 Listen to five dialogues in the departure lounge. Match the dialogues 1–5 to the letters A–E in the picture.

2 2.82 Listen to the dialogues again and answer the questions.

Dialogue 1
1 What is Frank going to do?
2 What kind of film is it?
Dialogue 2
3 Where is the man?
4 How is the man going to go to the hotel?
Dialogue 3
5 How long is the man going to be away?
6 How often is he going to call the woman?
Dialogue 4
7 Where is Nicky going?
8 Why is Esther going to Romania?
Dialogue 5
9 Where is the woman going?
10 What is the problem?

3 Look at audioscript 2.82 on page 126 and check your answers. Choose one dialogue and practise.

GRAMMAR: *going to* (1) future plans

Use *be going to* + verb to talk about future intentions.
*I'm **going to make** a film.*
*I'm **not going to take** these bags.*
***Are** you **going to call** me?*

SEE LANGUAGE REFERENCE PAGE 112

1 Make the sentences about the future.

1 clean the house (–) *I'm not going to clean the house.*
2 make a meal (+) *I'm going to make a meal.*
3 go away (–)
4 do the shopping (–)
5 visit friends (+)
6 see a film (+)
7 visit family (–)
8 stay at home (–)

2 Make questions with the phrases in exercise 1. Interview a partner about the weekend.

Are you going to clean the house? *Yes, I am.*

3 Complete the dialogues with *going to* and the verb in brackets.

A: Hi! What are you doing here?
B: I'm going to Siberia. My flight is in three hours.
A: Siberia?! What (1) _____ you _____ (*do*) in Siberia?
B: I (2) _____ (*speak*) at a conference. What about you?
A: I'm going to Italy. Again.
B: Family visit?
A: No, I (3) _____ (*not see*) my family this time. It's for work.

A: What's the purpose of your visit?
B: We (4) _____ (*visit*) friends.
A: Where (5) _____ you _____ (*stay*)?
B: At the Regent Hotel. Near the river.
A: OK, you can go.

SPEAKING

1 Work in pairs, A and B. You are friends. You meet at the airport terminal. Prepare a short dialogue.

2 2.83 Listen to the sound effects and have a dialogue about your future holiday.

Useful language

Hi! What are you doing here?
What are you going to do?
Where are you going to go?

ENGLISH AROUND YOU: at the airport

1 Look at some English words from the airport. What are these words in your language?

2 2.84 Listen and repeat the words.

3 Do you know any other international English words connected to transport?

12c | The end

Grammar: *Going to* (2); future time expressions
Vocabulary: Feelings
Functional language: Best wishes for the future

File Edit View Favourites Tools Help Links »

My blog

search

HOME ABOUT BLOG LINKS FAVOURITES SIGN-UP

JUNE 16

THE END OF THE COURSE!

Our course finished today. We all went to the park after the class and talked about our future plans. I'm a little sad because there aren't any more classes, but I'm happy because I have many new friends now. We're going to keep in touch, and of course we're going to see each other next year!

Here's a photo of all of us together.

I'm tired now, time for bed! Tomorrow we're going to have our final exam!

VIEW ALL BLOG ENTRIES

SPEAKING & READING

1 Work in pairs. Ask and answer the questions.

When does your English course finish?

Do you have a final exam?

What are you going to do after the course?

2 Read the blog above. What is it about, 1, 2 or 3?

1 the end of a course
2 the beginning of a course
3 a holiday

3 Read the blog again and answer the questions.

1 When did the course finish?
2 Why is the author happy?
3 When is the author going to see his friends again?
4 What is going to happen tomorrow?

VOCABULARY: feelings

1 Match the sentences 1–5 to the pictures A–E.

1 He's scared.
2 She's tired.
3 They're happy.
4 She's sad.
5 He's angry.

2 2.85 Listen and repeat.

3 Complete each sentence in two different ways.

I'm happy because …
I'm sad because …
I'm angry because …

GRAMMAR: *going to* (2); future time expressions

We can use these time expressions with the future.
tomorrow
tomorrow morning/evening
next Tuesday/week/month
They go at the beginning or end of a sentence.
We're going to see each other ***next year****.*
Tomorrow *we're going to have our final exam!*

SEE LANGUAGE REFERENCE PAGE 112

1 Put the time expressions on the diagram.

next Tuesday
next year
tonight
~~today~~
tomorrow evening
tomorrow morning
next month

2 Make questions with *going to* from the prompts.

1 you / travel next year?
Are you going to travel next year?
2 What / you / do next Friday?
3 Where / you / go after class?
4 you / study English next year?
5 you / come to school tomorrow?

3 2.86 Listen to some students talking at the end of their course. Check your answers to exercise 2.

PRONOUNCIATION: *going to*

1 2.87 Listen how some words are stressed more in these sentences.

What are you going to do?
Where are you going to go?
Are you going to call?

2 2.88 Listen to the questions in Grammar exercise 2 again. Underline the stressed words.

3 Work in pairs. Ask and answer the questions. Pay attention to the stressed words.

FUNCTIONAL LANGUAGE: best wishes for the future

1 2.89 Listen and repeat the phrases.

Have a nice holiday!
Good luck.
See you next year!

2 Look at the table. Choose one or two phrases and memorize them.

Have a nice	weekend.
	summer.
	holiday.
Good luck with	the exam.
	your new job.
See you next	week.
	course.
	September.

SPEAKING

1 Work in pairs, A and B. Have a dialogue. Follow the instructions.

A: Ask about B's future plans.
B: Say two things you are going to do. Ask about A's plans.
A: Answer B.
B: Give A best wishes.
A: Give B best wishes.
B: Say goodbye.
A: Say goodbye.

2 Close your books. Walk around the class and have a similar dialogue with two other people.

12D | Review

Speaking

1 Work in pairs. Prepare a phone dialogue. Use the diagram to help you.

A		B
Call B.	→	Answer the phone.
Say hello. Introduce yourself. Ask for C.	→	Say your name. Tell A that C isn't here. Offer to take a message.
Say your message.	→	Say OK.
Say thank you.	→	Respond.
Say goodbye.	→	Say goodbye.

Grammar

1 There is a word missing in each sentence. Insert the missing word.

1 I'm going to study English month.
2 I'm not going go away this weekend.
3 My family going to live in another country next year.
4 We going to have class next week.
5 The teacher not going to teach us next year.

2 Tick (✓) the sentences in exercise 1 that are true for you.

3 Work in pairs. Change the sentences in exercise 1 to questions. Ask and answer the questions.

Vocabulary

1 Play *Odd One Out*. Circle the wrong word in each group.

1	Beijing	Germany	Paris	Prague
2	four	seven	third	twelve
3	difficult	interesting	bad	bed
4	café	water	juice	tea
5	teacher	doctor	school	actor
6	red	medium	black	green
7	August	Monday	Wednesday	Friday
8	brother	mother	father	teacher
9	bridge	passport	supermarket	castle
10	cold	type	drive	sing

2 Work in pairs. Write your own *Odd One Out* exercise.

3 Work with another pair. Test each other.

Functional language

1 Match the expressions 1–8 to the pictures A–H on page 111.

1 What do you do?
2 What's this in English?
3 I'm sorry.
4 I'm just looking, thanks.
5 Excuse me.
6 What time is it?
7 How old is he?
8 Fine, thanks.

A

B

C

D

E

F

G

H

2 2.90 Listen to the recording to check your answers.

3 Choose one of the pictures. Cover the words and roleplay the situation.

Self-assessment (✓)

- ☐ I can answer the phone.
- ☐ I can leave a message on the phone.
- ☐ I can talk about future plans.

Grammar

Can/can't

Can is a modal auxiliary verb. We use it to talk about ability.

affirmative		
I You He/She/It We They	can	use a computer.
negative		
I You He/She/It We They	can't	use a computer.

I can speak French.
Not ~~*I can to speak English.*~~
I can't dance.
Not ~~*I don't can dance.*~~

question and short answer			
Can	I you he/she/it we they	dance?	
	Yes,	I you he/she/it we they	can.
	No,		can't.

Can you hear me?
Not ~~*Do you can hear me?*~~

Can has different uses.

Use *can* to talk about ability.
I can speak English.

Use can to ask for permission.
Can I use your phone?

Present continuous

Use the present continuous to talk about events happening now or around now.
To form the present continuous, we use the auxiliary verb *to be* in the present with the *-ing* form of the main verb.

affirmative			
full form		**contraction**	
I am You are He/She/It is We are They are	talking.	I'm You're He's/She's/It's We're They're	talking.

negative				
full form			**contraction**	
I am You are He/She/It is We are They are	not	listening.	I'm not You aren't He/She/It isn't We aren't They aren't	listening.

question	
Am I Are you Is he/she/it Are we Are they	listening?

Going to

Use *going to* + verb to talk about plans for the future.
She's ***going to visit*** *her parents in India.*

affirmative					
full form			**contraction**		
I am You are He/She/It is We are They are	going to	meet a friend.	I'm You're He's/She's/It's We're They're	going to	call.

negative						
full form				**contraction**		
I am You are He/She/It is We are They are	not	going to	have a holiday.	I'm not You aren't He/She/It isn't We aren't They aren't	going to	have a holiday.

question			short answer
Am I Are you Is he/she/it Are we Are they	going to	have a holiday?	Yes, I am. No, I'm not. Yes, you/they/we are. No, you/they/we aren't. Yes, he/she/it is. No, he/she/it isn't.

With the verb *go* you can say *I'm going to go to the party* OR *I'm going to the party.*

Future time expressions

We can use these time expressions with the future:

tomorrow
tomorrow morning/evening
next Monday/week/month/year
Not ~~*the next week*~~

next year
next month
next tuesday
tomorrow evening
tomorrow
tonight
today

Functional language

Talking about a painting

In this picture I can see a woman at a bar.
The flowers are yellow.
There are two boats on the river

Telephone English

Hello, this is Sandra.
Hello, it's Sandra.
Is that Mike?
Can I speak to Mike?
Is Mike there?

I'm sorry, Mike isn't here.
Can I take a message?
Would you like to call back?

Best wishes for the future

Have a nice holiday/weekend.
Good luck.
See you next year/month/September.

Word list

Action verbs

dance *v* ***	/dɑːns/
drive *v* ***	/draɪv/
play *v* ***	/pleɪ/
run *v* ***	/rʌn/
sing *v* ***	/sɪŋ/
swim *v* **	/swɪm/
type *v* *	/taɪp/
walk *v* ***	/wɔːk/

Telephoning

answer *v* ***	/ˈɑːnsə(r)/
call *v* ***	/kɔːl/
phone number *n* *	/ˈfəʊn ˌnʌmbə(r)/
send *v* ***	/send/
smartphone *n*	/ˈsmɑː(r)tˌfəʊn/
text message *n*	/tekst ˈmesɪdʒ/
turn off *v*	/ˌtɜː(r)n ˈɒf/
turn on *v*	/ˌtɜː(r)n ˈɒn/

Feelings

angry *adj* ***	/ˈæŋgri/
happy *adj* ***	/ˈhæpi/
sad *adj* ***	/sæd/
scared *adj* **	/skeː(r)d/
tired *adj* ***	/ˈtaɪə(r)d/

Other words & phrases

arrival *n* ***	/əˈraɪv(ə)l/
athlete *n* *	/ˈæθliːt/
blind *adj* **	/blaɪnd/
blog *n*	/blɒg/
cerebral palsy *n*	/ˌserəbrəl ˈpɔːlzi/
change *n* ***	/tʃeɪndʒ/
check-in *n*	/ˈtʃek ˌɪn/
competition *n* ***	/ˌkɒmpəˈtɪʃ(ə)n/
customs *n*	/ˈkʌstəmz/
deaf *adj* **	/def/
delayed *adj*	/dɪˈleɪd/
departure *n* **	/dɪˈpɑː(r)tʃə(r)/
disability *n* **	/ˌdɪsəˈbɪləti/
disabled *adj* **	/dɪsˈeɪb(ə)ld/
exam *n* **	/ɪgˈzæm/
find *v* ***	/faɪnd/
flight *n* ***	/flaɪt/
gallery *n* **	/ˈgæləri/
graphic artist *n*	/ˈgræfɪk ˈɑː(r)tɪst/
guitar *n* ***	/gɪˈtɑː(r)/
idea *n* ***	/aɪˈdɪə/
lounge *n* *	/laʊndʒ/
medal *n* **	/ˈmed(ə)l/
meeting *** *n*	/ˈmiːtɪŋ/
message *n* ***	/ˈmesɪdʒ/
model *n* ***	/ˈmɒd(ə)l/
noise *** *n*	/nɔɪz/
painting *n* ***	/ˈpeɪntɪŋ/
plans *n* ***	/plænz/
together *adj* ***	/təˈgeðə(r)/
vote *v* ***	/vəʊt/
wheelchair *n*	/ˈwiːlˌtʃeə(r)/

Communication activities

3A Speaking exercise 1 page 25

Student A

Read the information about the people.

Job File

Name	Country	Job	Phone number

Brad 	the US	architect	1 902 488 6521

Victor and Olga 	Russia	doctors	7 654 899 900

You start. Tell Student B about the people in your job file.

Listen to Student B talk about the people in his/her job file. Write the information in your job file.

5D Functional language exercise 1 page 49

Student B

Listen to Student A's addresses and write them down. If you don't understand, ask *How do you spell that?*

Read these email and website addresses to your partner.

martin991@mail.col

www.jobsincanada.col

hotel@online.col

www.visitlondon.col/information

11D Speaking exercise 1 page 103

Student A

Describe your picture to Student B. Find four differences in the pictures.

In my picture the man in the sunglasses is eating a sandwich.

4c Speaking exercise 1 page 37

Student A

Look at the picture. Don't show it to your partner.

Describe the picture to Student B.

Draw a …
Next to the … draw a …

7c Speaking exercise 1 page 65

Student B

You work at the tourist information office in Manhattan. Use the information for tourists below to help answer the tourist's questions.

Maps of Manhattan

colour map:	$5
black & white map:	$3.50

Tours

Central Park tour:	$17
Manhattan Movie tour:	$35
Statue of Liberty Boat tour:	$20

Broadway shows

Mamma Mia!
Phantom of the Opera
Chicago!

Special tickets:	$100

New York bus tours

Next bus tour: 5.15pm

7B Speaking exercise 1 page 63

Student A

10c Vocabulary exercise 4 page 90

Student A

Ask about the object.

How much is (the computer)?

Student B

Say the price.

It's ($699).

7c Speaking exercise 1 page 65

Student A

You are a tourist in New York City. You want information about these things:

- ☐ tour of Times Square?
- ☐ tickets to a Broadway show? / how much?
- ☐ a map of Manhattan? / how much?
- ☐ a bus tour? / what time?

If you don't understand, use the Functional language on page 64 to help you.

You start:

Excuse me, I'd like some information please.

10c Speaking exercise 1 page 91

Student B

You are a customer in the shop. Follow the instructions and have a dialogue with Student A.
Student A starts.

A:	
B: Respond. Ask for the price for something.	*Yes. How much is this …?*
A:	
B: Ask if you can pay by credit card.	*Can I pay by credit card?*
A:	
B: Say thank you. Give the card.	*Thanks. Here you are.*
A:	
B: Accept.	*Yes, please.*
A:	
B: Say goodbye.	*Goodbye.*

Cover the words on the right above. Repeat the dialogue.

7B Speaking exercise 1 page 63

Student B

5D Functional language exercise 1 page 49

Student A

Read the email and website addresses to your partner.

www.maximum.col

sarah@hotmail.col

info@english.co.ur

www.sandwich.col/drinks

Listen to Student B's addresses and write them down. If you don't understand, ask, *How do you spell that?*

4C Speaking exercise 1 page 37

Student B

Look at the picture. Don't show it to your partner.

Describe the picture to Student A.

Draw a …
Next to the … draw a …

10D Speaking exercise 2 page 93

A

B

C

D

E

F

G

H

11A Reading exercise 3 page 96

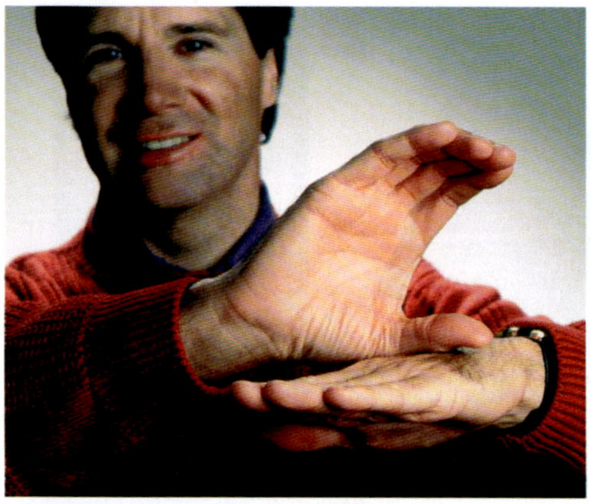

Nathan
He's deaf. He can't hear.

Janice
She's blind. She can't see.

Isaac
He uses a wheelchair. He can't walk.

3A Speaking exercise 1 page 25

Student B

Read the information about the people.

Job File

Name	Country	Job	Phone number
Michael 	Britain	student	44 93 657 8845

Kanako 	Japan	teacher	81 3 3499 8254

Student A starts. Listen to Student A talk about the people in his/her job file. Write the information in your job file.

Tell Student A about the people on your job file.

10C Speaking exercise 1 page 91

Student A

You work in the shop. Follow the instructions and have a dialogue with Student B. You start.

A: Ask B if he/she wants help.	*Can I help you?*
B:	
A: Tell B the price.	*It's … dollars, please.*
B:	
A: Accept. Take B's card.	*Yes, of course.*
B:	
A: Offer B a bag.	*Would you like a bag?*
B:	
A: Say thank you and goodbye.	*Thank you. Goodbye.*
B:	

Cover the words on the right. Repeat the dialogue.

11D Speaking exercise 1 page 103

Student B

Describe your picture to Student A. Find four differences in the pictures.

In my picture the people are dancing.

2C Functional language exercise 2 page 19

Work in pairs. Make dialogues with the words and pictures.

coffee: black or white?

juice: apple or orange?

mineral water: sparkling or still?

Audioscripts

1B Listening exercises 1 & 2 1.9

1 My name is Polly. I'm from Britain.
2 This is Pierre. He's from Paris, France.
3 Her name's Sofia. She's from Italy.
4 His name's Michael. He's from the US.
5 Where are you from?
We're from Germany.
6 This is Nikita and Igor. They're from Russia.

1C Vocabulary exercise 2 1.13

1 beep beep
2 beep beep beep beep
3 beep
4 beep beep beep beep beep
5 beep beep beep beep beep beep beep beep beep
6 beep beep beep

1C Listening exercises 1 & 2 1.14

1 **M = man W = woman**

M: Oh, just a second … err … sorry … a missed call.
W: You have one call from 623 485 531.

2 **W = woman W2 = woman 2**

W: So, is there a message, any messages for me?
W2: Yes, James called.
W: Ahh. Did he leave a number?
W2: Yes. 945 0782. It's on the table.

3 **M = man**

M: Yes … err … can you call Mrs Kirsch and tell her she has a place in the 7pm … err … yes, 7pm English class? Her name is Kirsch and her number is 321 4510. Again, that's 321 4510.

4 **W = woman**

W: YES! Call our free number now for more information! The number is 1 888 962 962. That's 1 888 962 962. Call now.

1D Functional language exercise 2 1.20

1 **M = man**

M: Hello!

2 **W = woman**

W: Goodbye!

3 **M1 = man 1 M2 = man 2**

M1: Nice to meet you.
M2: Nice to meet you, too.

4 **M1 = man 1 M2 = man 2**

M1: Hi! How are you?
M2: I'm fine. And you?
M1: Fine, thanks.

2A Listening exercise 2 1.21

R = receptionist T = Tom

R: Hello. Welcome to our hotel, the best hotel in Bangkok, Thailand!
T: Hello. I have a reservation.
R: What's your name, please?
T: I'm Tom and this is Katy.
R: What's your last name?
T: Crewes.
R: Excuse me, Cruise?
T: Not the actor. My name's C-R-E-W-E-S.

2A Vocabulary & pronunciation exercise 5 1.25

1 **M = man R = receptionist**

M: My name is Tom Crewes.
R: How do you spell your last name?
M: C-R-E-W-E-S.
R: Oh. Thank you.

2 **R = receptionist K = Kate**

R: Welcome to our hotel.
V: I have a reservation. My name is Kate MIddledown.
R: Excuse me? Middleton?
V: No, Middledown.
R: How do you spell your name?
V: M-I-D-D-L-E-D-O-W-N.

2A Vocabulary & listening exercise 2 1.28

M = man Y = Ying

M: Hello, Ying. How are you?
Y: Fine, thanks. And you?
M: I'm fine. Listen, I'm just checking the hotel rooms.
Y: OK. Mr Crewes is in room 14.
M: Yes.
Y: Mrs MIddledown is …
M: Mrs Middleton?
Y: No, MiddleDOWN. She's in room 17.
M: And Mr and Mrs Bickham?
Y: In room 20.
M: Good.
Y: And Mr Clunie is in room 11.
M: Wonderful. Good work, Ying.
Y: Thank you.

2A English around you exercise 2 1.30

BBC British Broadcasting Corporation
IBM International Business Machines
CNN Cable News Network
UK United Kingdom
US United States
FBI Federal Bureau of Investigation

2C Listening exercise 1 1.35

W = waitress M1 = man 1 M2 = man 2
Wo1 = woman 1 Wo2 = woman 2 F = Frank

W: Yes?
M1: I'd like two coffees, please.
W: Two coffees, OK.

Wo1: A tea and a croissant, please.
W: OK.
M2: Excuse me?
W: Yes?
M2: Two sandwiches.
W: Would you like cheese or tuna?
M2: Cheese sandwiches, please.
Wo2: Hello.
W: Hi.
Wo2: I'd like two teas, please, over here.
W: OK, Frank? Two coffees, three teas, a croissant and two cheese sandwiches!
F: OK!

2D Listening exercise 1 1.40

1 **M = man W = woman**

M: So, where are you from?
W: Cambridge.
M: How do you spell that?
W: C-A-M-B-R-I-D-G-E.

2 **W = woman M = man**

W: The hotel … ahh … it's wonderful.
M: Where is it?
W: In Torquay.
M: Where?
W: T-O-R-Q-U-A-Y. Torquay.

3 **W = woman M = man**

W: Mmmm … good cheese.
M: Where is it from?
W: Cheshire.
M: C-H-E-S-H-I-R-E?
W: Yes, that's right.

4 **M = man W = woman**

M: Write this down.
W: OK.
M: Greenwich. That's G-R-E-E-N-W-I-C-H. In London.
W: OK, Greenwich.

3B Listening exercises 1 & 2 1.48

M = Mike D = Dominique

M: Whew. Well. Hello.
D: Hello.
M: Do you speak English?
D: Yes. A little.
M: My name's Mike.
D: I'm Dominique. Nice to meet you.
M: Nice to meet you, too. Where are you from in France?
D: Oh, I'm not French. I'm from Switzerland.
M: Ah. Sorry.
D: It's OK. Where are you from?
M: The US.
D: Mmm.
M: Excuse me?
D: Yes?
M: What time do we arrive in Madrid?
D: Madrid?
M: Yes.
D: Oh no. This train is for Milan.
M: What? But this is the Spanish Express to Madrid.
D: No, no, no. This train isn't the Spanish Express to Madrid. This train is the Italian Express. The next stop is Milan.
M: Oh no!

3C Listening exercises 1 & 2 1.53

M1 = man 1 W1 = woman 1
W2 = woman 2 M2 = man 2

M1: And that's the end of our tour of UNIS, the United Nations International School. Any questions? Yes?
W1: When is the school open?
M1: The school is open Monday to Saturday.
M2: Is the school cafeteria open every day?
M1: No, it isn't. The cafeteria isn't open on Saturdays.
W1: Where are the teachers from?
M1: Many teachers at UNIS are from the United States, but we also have French, German, Swiss, Italian, Japanese and Australian teachers.
W2: Are you the Director?
M1: No I'm not. I'm the Assistant Director.
W1: Who is the Director?
M1: The Director is Mr Stuart Walker. He's in his office right now.

4A Listening exercises 1 & 2 1.62

1 **M1 = man 1 M2 = man 2**

M1: Hey, is that a photo of your car?
M2: Yes, it is.
M1: How old is it?
M2: Well … it's forty-five years old.
M1: Mmm … very nice.
M2: Thank you.

2 **W = woman M = man**

W: What a beautiful photo! Are they your babies?
M: Yes. This is Fabio, this is Fiona and that's Lea.
W: Beautiful! How old are they?
M: In this photo? They're eighteen months old.
W: Awww. So young!

3 **M = man W = woman**

M: So … here's a photo of the house I'm thinking of.
W: Well, come on. Let's see.
M: It's not a new house …
W: How old is this house?
M: One hundred and … twelve years old.

4 **W = woman M = man**

W: We need to choose a new computer.
M: How about this one? Look at the picture.
W: Mmm. This isn't new.
M: It's not new. No. It's from the London office.
W: Oh.
M: It's nine months old. We don't have money for a new computer.
W: Oh. Well, OK, then. Nine months old. OK.

4C Listening exercises 1 & 2 1.71

L = Lee M = Mark

1
L: Hi, Mark.
M: Oh, hello.

L: Umm ... where's my bag?
M: What?
L: My bag. My black bag.
M: I think it's on the table.
L: OK. No, it isn't.
M: Is it under the table, then?
L: Oh, yes, here it is.
M: Good.

2

L: Mark?
M: What is it?
L: Where are my glasses?
M: They're in your black bag.
L: No, they aren't.
M: In your jacket?
L: What jacket?
M: Your brown jacket. On the chair.
L: Oh, yes, here they are.
M: Good.

3

L: Mark?
M: What now?
L: Where's my wallet?
It isn't in my brown jacket.
It isn't on the table.
It isn't in my bag.
M: I don't know where your wallet is! OK?
L: OK, OK.
Oh, look! Here it is. It's on the sofa. Next to you.
M: Fine, here.
L: Thanks, Mark. Bye.
M: Bye.

4D Listening exercises 2 & 3 1.72

Who is Lindsay? Hi, I'm Lindsay. I'm married and I'm 40. I'm an English teacher. I'm from Toronto, Canada. My family is from England. I'm the author of *Straightforward Beginner Second edition*. It's a book for English language students. Where is Lindsay now? In Spain.

5B Listening exercises 1 & 2 1.77

1 W = woman J = Jeffrey

W: I use email all the time. Not personal emails, though. Only emails for work. What about you, Jeffrey?
J: Oh, I don't know anything about computers or technology. I don't use emails, or the internet, or digital cameras.
W: No internet? Really? You're a bit anti-technology.
J: I have a mobile phone, but it's my brother's old mobile phone.

2 M = man W = woman

M: My wife knows all about computers. She works in an office.
W: Mmm.
M: She has, I think, two or three computers at work.
W: Two or three?
M: Yes, yes. We don't have a computer at home. She doesn't work at home ... so no computer.

3 M = man W = woman

M: What's this? Is it an e-book?
W: No, it isn't. It's a tablet computer. We use it at the school.
M: A tablet computer. Is it only for the teacher?
W: No. All the students have them now. The students and the teacher use them. We don't use computers in the computer room now.
M: Oh.

5D Vocabulary exercise 3 1.84

M = man W = woman

1

M: OK, I'll give you my email address.
W: Just a minute. My pen ... OK.
M: My email address is ... it's hal006 at mail dot com.
W: Sorry, again?
M: H-a-l-0-0-6 at mail, m-a-i-l dot com.
W: Good. Thank you.

2 M = man W = woman

W: It's easier if you email me.
M: OK, what's your email address?
W: Sofia, that's s-o-f-i-a at i-a dot net.
M: I-a dot net. OK.

3

For more information, email us. Our email is mercedes at k-a-r dot com.

6B Listening exercises 1 & 2 1.92

M = man W = woman

M: Hello, the Community Centre? Edward speaking.
W: Hello, I'd like some information about the chess club, please.
M: Of course.
W: When does it meet?
M: Every Saturday. In the morning.
W: OK, Saturday morning. Err .. what time does it start?
M: At ten o'clock.
W: And ... how much is it?
M: It's five pounds for the month.
W: Five pounds. OK, thank you.
M: Anything else?
W: Oh, yes. One more thing. Who do I talk to about the language classes?
M: Call the language school information number. It's 9023.
W: Thank you.
M: You're welcome. Goodbye.
W: Bye.

6C Reading & listening exercises 2 & 3 2.2

I = interviewer M = man

I: Hi, excuse me. I'm doing a survey on eating habits. Can I ask you some questions?
M: Errr ... yes, OK.
I: Thanks. First question: do you have three meals a day?
M: Do you mean like breakfast, lunch and dinner? Yes, I do.
I: OK. Question 2. Do you eat fruit and/or vegetables every day?
M: Mmm. Yes, I do. I eat an apple every day.
I: Do you eat meat and/or fish every day?
M: No, I don't. My wife is a vegetarian. I eat meat once a week, maybe.
I: How often do you have a meal at a restaurant?
M: Three, maybe four times a year.
I: How often do you eat with your family?
M: We have dinner together every night.

I: How often do you have lunch at work or school?
M: Well … I eat at home on Friday, but the other days I eat at work. So four times a week.

6D Vocabulary & listening exercise 2 2.5

1
Right, this morning we have eggs, toast, an apple or an orange, or a croissant.

2 W = woman M = man

W: What's on the menu, please?
M: Err … soup – chicken or vegetable, a sandwich – cheese or tuna, fish or pasta of the day.
W: Oh.

6D Vocabulary & listening exercises 3 & 4 2.6

B = Ben Bk = Becky

B: Hello, Becky.
Bk: Hi there, Ben.
B: What time is it, Becky?
Bk: Errr … one o'clock.
B: Mmm. Time for lunch.
Bk: What would you like, Ben?
B: I'd like the soup.
Bk: Would you like chicken or vegetable?
B: Vegetable … no. Chicken, please.
Bk: OK, chicken soup. And …?
B: And the fish, please.
Bk: Chicken soup and fish. OK, Ben.
B: Thanks, Becky.

7C Listening exercises 2 & 3 2.15

1 W = woman M = man

W: Hello.
M: Hi, can I help you?
W: Yes, what time is the next city tour of York?
M: The next one is at a quarter to four.
W: I'm sorry, I don't speak English very well. Can you repeat that, please?
M: A quarter to four. Three forty-five.
W: Thank you.

2 M = man W = woman

M: Excuse me, is this the tourist information office?
W: Yes, it is.
M: I'd like two tickets for the Mystery Play tonight.
W: It's sold out.
M: I'm sorry, I don't understand.
W: There aren't any tickets for the play today. Come back on Friday.
M: On Friday? Oh, thank you.
W: You're welcome. Goodbye.

3 M = man W = woman

M: Hello, is this the Jorvik Centre?
W: Excuse me?
M: Is this the Jorvik Centre?
W: I'm sorry. I only speak a little English. I'm not from here.
M: OK. Thank you.

4 M1 = man 1 M2 = man 2

M1: Excuse me, I don't speak English very well. Do you speak Spanish?
M2: No, I'm sorry, I don't.
M1: Is the castle near here?
M2: Yes, it is. Do you have a map?
M1: Yes, here.
M2: Well, look. We're here … and the castle is over there.
M1: OK, thank you!
M2: You're welcome. Err … adios … heh, heh!

7D Listening exercise 2 2.22

1
Aha, there's the map! What do you think is the best route then?

2 W = woman M = man

W: Excuse me?
M: Yes?
W: Your passport, please.
M: Who are you? What is this?
W: Police. Your passport, please, sir.

3 M = man W = woman

M: So … ready, darling?
W: Yes, I think so. Urgh. Yep! Ready!
M: Is that *your* luggage?
W: Yes, darling. Why?
M: It's just that … it's a lot of luggage.
W: Yes, darling. It's our holiday!

4 M = man W = woman

M: Excuse me?
W: Kann ich Ihnen helfen?
M: I'm sorry. I don't understand.
W: Kann ich Ihnen helfen?
M: I'd like an English-German phrase book.
W: Sorry, can you repeat, please?
M: An English-German phrase book. So I can understand you.

8C Pronunciation exercises 1 & 2 2.30

1 It's good.
2 These are great.
3 It's awful.
4 It's bad.

8C Listening exercises 1 & 2 2.31

1 W = woman M = man

W: What kind of food do you like?
M: Err, Chinese food. I love it. There's a Chinese restaurant near my house that has great dinners. It's good.

2 W1 = woman 1 W2 = woman 2

W1: These are great.
W2: What are?
W1: The new computers. I love them. They're so easy. And beautiful.
W2: I know.

3 M = man W = woman

M: What do you think of the film *Robot Attack*?
W: Oh, please.

M: What?
W: It's bad. No, sorry, it's not just bad. It's awful!
M: Do you like the actor?
W: I don't know him. But science fiction films. Urgh. I don't like them.

9c Listening exercises 2 & 3 2.42

C = Charlie S = Sandra

C: July 4th is Independence Day in the United States. We got our independence from England on this day in 1776. In my town there is an Independence Day parade, with music and flags. Same old story every year. I hardly ever go to the parade. But I always have a big barbecue with friends and family. A typical American barbecue, with hamburgers and cola. After the barbecue we often play a game of baseball. It's a great day. A great day just to be with friends and family, really.
S: In Mexico we have lots of holidays. Our national holiday, our celebration of independence, is in September. It celebrates the beginning of our fight for independence from Spain on September 16th, 1810. On this day I don't go to work. I usually have a big meal with my family in the evening. Then we go to the main square, the zocalo, for *el grito*. All the people shout 'Viva Mexico!'. There is always music and dancing. The party goes on very late into the night. Our independence day is never boring. I like it very much.

9c Functional language exercise 3 2.45

1 What's the third month?
2 What's the eighth month?
3 What's the first month?
4 What's the eleventh month?
5 What's the sixth month?
6 What's the second month?

9d Listening exercise 1 2.48

A Hard Day's Night – The Beatles by numbers!
The Beatles made an amazing number of songs. In total they had 217 songs, including 59 singles. There are at least 77 Beatles CDs. The Beatles played in 1,400 live concerts.
And they hold the world record for most sales of an album. Their greatest hits album, *1*, sold more than thirteen million copies in the first month.

9d Grammar exercise 2 2.49

1 He worked in a factory.
2 We hated the film.
3 I play tennis, watch TV …
4 The teacher wanted an answer.
5 She danced all night.

10a Listening exercises 1 & 2 2.51

W = woman M = man

W: Hi, John. How are you? You know, I had a really great weekend. Do you want to hear about it?
M: OK.
W: But you first. How was your weekend?
M: It was fine.
W: What did you do?
M: Oh, I did nothing much.
W: Oh, well, because I …
M: I woke up late, cleaned the car …
W: Really? Interesting.
M: … did the shopping.
W: Mmm. Fantastic.
M: I watched TV.
W: TV. Great.
M: I saw the football match.
W: Do you want to know what I did this weekend?
M: What did you do?
W: I went away. To France. I went with Jacques.
M: Really. Did you have a good time?
W: Oh, it was great. We went to Paris. I loved it. He loved it. Would you like to see my photos?
M: No, thank you.

10a Grammar exercise 1 2.54

1 Did you go to the cinema last night?
2 Did you see a football match last night?
3 Did you read a book last night?
4 Did you go to a party last night?

10b Listening exercises 2 & 3 2.56

OK, OK. Quiet please. Ready for the quiz. These questions are multiple choice. I'll read the question and the possible answers. The first question is History. When did Neil Armstrong walk on the moon?
Was it …
a) on July 20th 1969?
b) on June 1st 1969?
c) on July 1st 1991?
The next section is Sports. Where were the first modern Olympic Games?
a) Paris.
b) Athens.
c) New York.
Section three. Science and Nature. Where did potatoes originally come from?
a) Asia.
b) Latin America.
c) Europe.
Section four is Film. Our question here is: Who was the first James Bond?
a) Sean Connery.
b) Daniel Craig.
c) Roger Moore.
The last section is Music. Ready? When did the Beatles break up?
a) 1972.
b) 1970.
c) 1971.

10b Pronunciation exercise 1 2.57

1 Where did Mozart come from?
2 Who was the author of *Romeo and Juliet*?
3 When did Brazil get its independence?

4 What is the capital of Austria?
5 Who is the President of Russia?

10C Listening exercises 1 & 2 2.60

SA = sales assistant C = customer
M = man W = woman

1
SA: Hello, can I help you?
C: I'm just looking, thanks.

2
C: Excuse me?
SA: Yes?
C: Where are the changing rooms?

3
M: How much is this?
SA: It's six hundred pounds.
W: I love it.
M: Can I pay by credit card?

4
SA: Would you like a bag for that?
C: Yes, please.

10D Vocabulary exercise 1 2.61

1 **SA = sales assistant C = customer**
SA: That's sixteen fifty, please.
C: Sixteen dollars … and fifty cents. Here you are.

2 **SA = sales assistant C = customer**
SA: It's two thousand euros.
C: Two thousand? For shoes?
SA: They are very good shoes, madam.

3 **Ch = child M = man**
Ch: How much is that sweet there?
M: Eighty p.
Ch: Oh. I only have fifty p.
M: Sorry.

4
On sale now, all CDs for one ninety-nine, that's one pound ninety-nine!

11A Pronunciation exercise 2 2.66

1 Can you swim?
2 Yes, I can.
3 No, I can't.
4 I can't dance.
5 I can dance.

11B Listening exercises 1 & 2 2.68

1 **M = man W = woman**
M: Hello?
W: Hi! Where are you?
M: I'm in the car. I can't talk now, though, I'm driving.
W: I'm at the front gates. I have the tickets.
M: OK. See you, bye!

2 **W = woman J = Josh**
W: Josh?
J: Hello?
W: Josh, what are you doing? We're waiting for you!
J: I'm getting something to eat.
W: What? I can't hear a thing.
J: I'm eating! I'll be there in a minute.

3 **R = Rob Mi = Michelle**
R: Michelle?
Mi: Rob? Where are you? I can't see you.
R: I'm standing over here, near the stage. I can see you! Over here!
Mi: Where?
R: I'm wearing my red jacket! You're looking at me now!
Mi: Oh yes, there you are! OK, I'm coming over now.

4 **W = woman M = man**
W: Hello?
M: Hi. Are you at the office?
W: No, I'm not working today. I'm at Glastonbury.
M: Glastonbury? How is it? Is it raining?
W: Yes, it is. As usual. But we're having a good time, anyway.
M: Oh. Well, call me tonight, OK?
W: Sure.

11B English around you exercise 1 2.73

Fairtrade Foundation
International Committee of the Red Cross
Greenpeace
Save the Children

11C Listening exercises 1 & 2 2.74

This painting is one of the most popular in Britain. Vincent Van Gogh painted these flowers when he was in France. The flowers are yellow, a symbol of happiness. Van Gogh painted more than eleven paintings with sunflowers.

In this painting I can see a woman. She is working in a bar in Paris. The amazing thing about this painting is the woman's eyes. I can't say how she is feeling. Maybe she's sad. Maybe she doesn't want to work there. There are lots of people behind her. They are drinking and having a good time.

The Temeraire was a famous warship in English history. In this painting we can see a small boat in front of *The Temeraire*. The small boat is pulling the big boat. The colour of the sun and the sea is very dramatic here. I really like this painting.

11D Listening exercises 1 & 2 2.76

M = man W = woman
M: Hello. Good morning.
W: Good morning.
M: I'm here for the job interview.
W: Ah yes, yes. The job interview. Of course, come in.
M: Thanks.
W: Right. OK. I have some questions for you.
M: Fine.
W: Can you sing?
M: Sorry?
W: Sing … sing, you know, la la la.
M: Err … no, I can't. Not very well, no.

W: Oh. Can you dance?
M: What? Just a minute …
W: Answer the question, please, yes or no. Can you dance?
M: No, I can't.
W: You can't dance and you can't sing. What are you doing here?
M: I'm here for the tourist information job.
W: Tourist information job? Oh no. That job interview is in room 4. This is room 3. This room is for television actor interviews.
M: Ah, sorry.
W: That's OK. Goodbye, then.
M: Goodbye.

12A Listening exercises 2 & 3 2.78

C = Clark SG = security guard M = man
P = Paula S = Sara

1

C: Hmm … come on, Sara, where are you?
SG: Excuse me.
C: Yes?
SG: You can't use the mobile phone in the building.
C: Sorry.
M: Hello.
C: Yes, can I speak to Sara, please?
M: I'm sorry, you have the wrong number. There's no Sara here. This is McDonald's©.
C: Sorry …

2

P: Hello?
C: Hi. Is that Sara?
P: No, it's Paula.
C: Hi Paula, this is Clark. Can I speak to Sara, please?
P: Just a minute.
I'm sorry, Sara isn't here. She isn't at work today. Can I take a message?
C: Yes. Please tell her Clark called.
P: OK.
C: Thanks, bye.
P: Bye.

3

S: Hello.
C: Is that Sara?
S: Hi, Clark.
C: Sara, where are you?
S: I'm at home. Why?
C: Well, I'm at the library. I'm waiting for you!
S: Oh no! I'm sorry. I forgot!
C: Doh!
S: I'll be there in half an hour.
C: Oh … all right, then.

12B Listening exercises 1 & 2 2.82

1 **J = Jenny F = Frank**

J: Frank, I'm Jenny from the Entertainment news.
F: Hi Jenny.
J: What are you doing here, Frank?
F: I'm going to make a film here.
J: What film?
F: It's a remake of a Hitchcock film.

2 **W = woman M = man**

W: Where are you?
M: I'm at the airport.
W: Good.
M: What do I do now?
W: Go outside the terminal. A car is waiting for you. It's going to take you to your hotel.
M: Right.

3 **W = woman Ja = James**

W: Oh, James.
Ja: Darling.
W: Am I going to see you again, James?
Ja: Yes, darling. It's only a week.
W: Are you going to call me?
Ja: Yes, darling. Every night.

4 **N = Nicky E = Esther**

N: Esther!
E: Nicky! What are you doing here?
N: I'm going to Bangkok.
E: Bangkok?
N: Yes, I'm going to see a friend. And you?
E: I'm going to visit my father in Romania.

5 **SG = security guard W = woman**

SG: Excuse me, you can't leave your bags here.
W: It's just for a minute. I'm going to use the toilet.
SG: Please take your bags with you.
W: I'm not going to take these big bags into the toilet!
SG: I'm sorry, madam, but these are the rules.

12C Grammar exercise 3 2.86

1 **W = woman M = man**

W: Anyway, this summer I'm going to visit my family. They're in France.
M: That sounds nice.
W: What about you? Are you going to travel next year?
M: Me? No, I'm not. I'm going to stay here.

2 **M = man W = woman**

M: What are you going to do next Friday?
W: I don't have any plans. Why?
M: We're going to see the new Brad Pitt film. Would you like to come?
W: Yes, sure.

3 **W = woman M = man**

W: Where are you going to go after class?
M: To the library. I'm going to study.

4 **M = man W = woman**

M: Are you going to study English next year?
W: No, I'm not.
M: Oh no, why not?
W: I'm going to live in England. I've got a job there for next August.
M: Wow.

5 **M = man W = woman**

M: Are you going to come to school tomorrow?
W: Yes! We're going to take the exam. Don't you remember?
M: Oh yes, that's right.

Irregular verb list

Infinitive	Past simple	Translation
be***	was/were	________
become***	became	________
break***	broke	________
build***	built	________
buy***	bought	________
catch***	caught	________
choose***	chose	________
come***	came	________
cost***	cost	________
cut***	cut	________
do***	did	________
drink***	drank	________
drive***	drove	________
eat***	ate	________
fall***	fell	________
feel***	felt	________
find***	found	________
fly***	flew	________
forget***	forgot	________
get***	got	________
give***	gave	________
go***	went	________
have***	had	________
hear***	heard	________
hit***	hit	________
keep***	kept	________
know***	knew	________
learn***	learnt	________
make***	made	________
meet***	met	________
pay***	paid	________
put***	put	________
read***	read	________
ride**	rode	________
run***	ran	________
say***	said	________
see***	saw	________
sell***	sold	________
send***	sent	________
shut***	shut	________
sit***	sat	________
smell*	smelt	________
speak***	spoke	________
spend***	spent	________
stand***	stood	________
swim**	swam	________
take***	took	________
tell***	told	________
win***	won	________

Macmillan Education
Between Towns Road, Oxford OX4 3PP
A division of Macmillan Publishers Limited

Companies and representatives throughout the world

ISBN 978-0-230-42295-7 Student's Book
ISBN 978-0-230-42444-9 Student's Book & website access

This edition published 2013
First edition published 2007

This edition designed by eMC Design Limited
Original design by Oliver Design
Illustrated by Rowan Barnes-Murphy (illustrationOnLine.com) p46; Humberto Blanco (Sylvie Poggio Artists Agency) p106; Fred Blunt (Beehive Illustration) pp99, 104, 105cl; Anne Cakebread (The Art Market) pp39, 52, 62, 70, 115tr, 116; Seb Camagajevac (Beehive Illustration) pp7tc, 8, 9, 10l, 11tl, 15, 19, 29, 33l, 51, 53, 59, 64, 72, 77, 91r, 105tl, 109; Cyrus Deboo pp40, 52, 60, 96, 119r; Mark Duffin pp10r, 11br, 16, 20–21, 30l, 52, 115br; Abel Ippolito (Beehive Illustration) pp13l, 27, 35tl, 56l, 85l, 102, 108; Joanna Kerr (Meiklejohn Illustration) pp17, 26, 33r, 35br, 36, 50, 67, 115tl, 117; Peter Lubach (Beehive Illustration) pp13r, 22, 30r, 91l, 114, 119l; Sarah Nayler (NB Illustration) pp7cl, 12, 37, 56r, 75, 87, 105r, 111
Cover design by eMC Design Limited
Cover photograph by Getty Images/Doug Chinnery (main); Alamy/Robert Harding Picture Library Ltd; Corbis/Roger Tidman; Corbis/Lois Ellen Frank; Corbis/Gerolf Kalt; Alamy/Images & Stories.
Picture research by Susannah Jayes

Authors' acknowledgements
Lindsay would like to thank Philip Kerr for believing in him at the very beginning. As always, a great thank you must go to my wife Sofia and my children Lucas and Marcos for all their support.

The publishers would like to thank all the teachers from around the world who provided invaluable comments, suggestions and feedback on the first edition. The publishers would also like to thank the following people for their help and contribution to the second edition:
Tatiana Baytimerova (Russia), Lenka Boehmová (Czech Republic), Dr. Manuel Padilla Cruz (Spain), Svetlana Elchaninova (Russia), Jennifer Díaz Green (Dublin), Elena Mokeeva (Romania), Lynn Thomson (freelance editor), Amany Shawkey (Macmillan Egypt), Maria Teresa Rius Villaplana (Spain), Natalia Vorobyeva (Russia).

The authors and publishers would like to thank the following for permission to reproduce their photographs:
Alamy/AKP Photos p63(b), Alamy/Ambrophoto p54(tml), Alamy/Blend Images pp47(bcrr), 86(B), Alamy/Mark Boulton p64(A), Alamy/Candy Box Photography p66(cl), Alamy/Captured Sight p64(b), Alamy/Catchlight Visual Services p114(bl), Alamy/Cephas Picture Library p64(B), Alamy/Bernhard Classen p27, Alamy/Stuart Craig p26(B), Alamy/Tom Craig p26(E), Alamy/Sam Edwards p34(tcr), Alamy/Fancy p66(cml), Alamy/Stan Fellerman p9(D), Alamy/Filaphoto p44(B), Alamy/Paul Fleet p44(A), Alamy/Hemis p12(tcr), Alamy/David Hoffman Photo Library p48(bl), Alamy/D. Hurst pp17(bmr),93(D),117(D), Alamy/Ice Tea Media p34(cr), Alamy/imagebroker pp12(cr), 24(B), Alamy/Image Source pp17(bcr), 24(B), Alamy/INTERFOTO p61(tml), Alamy/Jewellery Specialist pp93(H), 117(H), Alamy/Juice Images p114(tcl), Alamy/Russell Kard p47(cmr), Alamy/Lenscap p20(tl), Alamy/Mark Leonard pp98–99(b), Alamy/Richard Levine p82(A), Alamy/LJSPhotography p47(bcr), Alamy/© Oleksiy Maksymenko Photography pp44(G), 93(C), 117(C), Alamy/Silas Manhood p54(tcl), Alamy/Ekateriana Minaeva pp93(G), 117(G), Alamy/MIXA pp93(A), 117(A), Alamy/Mode Images p17(tcr), Alamy/Nikreates p44(D), Alamy/Ian Nolan p17(cr,cmr), Alamy/David Norton p90(bl), Alamy/Mikhail Olykaynen p66(B), Alamy/PhotoAlto p9(A), Alamy/Andres Rodriguez p9(C), Alamy/Grant Rooney p90(br), Alamy/Sherab p26(A), Alamy/Alexander Shuldiner p61(cr), Alamy/John Simmons p9(B), Alamy/Danny Smythe p54(tcmll), Alamy/Stockshoot p26(F), Alamy/Mark Sykes, York UK p64(C), Alamy/Phil Talbot p32(C), Alamy/third cross pp93(F), 117(F), Alamy/Art Directors and Trip p44(H), Alamy/John Vincent p14(tl), Alamy/Jackie Weisberg p39(bl), Alamy/Elizabeth Whiting and Associates p44(C), Alamy/Bill Wymar p64(D), Alamy/Zoonar GmbH p54(tmll); **Apple Inc** pp17(tmr),32(A), 44(F); **Brand X** p54(bcl); **Bridgeman Art Library**/*Automat*, 1927, Edward Hopper (1882–1967)/Des Moines Art Center, Des Moines, Iowa, USA p101, Bridgeman Art Library/*Sunflowers*, 1888, Vincent van Gogh (1853–90)/National Gallery, London, UK p100(bl), Bridgeman Art Library/*The Fighting Temeraire*, 1839, Joseph Mallord William Turner (1775–1851)/National Gallery, London, UK p100(br), Bridgeman Art Library/*Café Terrace*, Place du Forum, Arles, Vincent van Gogh (1853–90)/Rijksmuseum Kroller-Muller, Otterlo, Netherlands p103(A), Bridgeman Art Library/*A Bar at the Folies-Bergere*, 1881–82, Edouard Manet (1832–83) © Samuel Courtauld Trust, The Courtauld Gallery, London, UK p100(cr); **www.cartoonstock.com**/Giles Pilbrow p63(cr); **Lindsay Clandfield** p38(tl); **Corbis** p8(br), Corbis/Atlantide Phototravel p79(tl), Corbis/Heide Benser p79(br), Corbis/Bettmann p103(B), Corbis/Howard Deshong, the food passionates p18(H), Corbis/David J. Frent p81(cmr), Corbis/Erik Isakson p84(tr), Corbis/ Whisson/Jarden p114(cl), Corbis/Luke Jarvis p104, Corbis/Martin Jones p32(D), Corbis/Katherine Karnow p61(bmll), Corbis/Mark Karrass p110, Corbis/Richard Morell p24(E), Corbis/Nossa Productions p47(bmr), Corbis/Ocean pp32(A), 43(B), Corbis/Paul Thompson p20(bl), Corbis/Claudia Rehm/Westend 61 p34(tcl), Corbis/Per Winbladh p24(C); **Digital Vision** p54(cml); **Fairtrade Foundation** p99(tmr); **Getty Images** pp54(tcml), 69, 74(cl), 80, 89(cr), 108, Getty Images/AFP pp43(A), 83, Getty Images/AlexandraR pp38–39(b), Getty Images/Tony Anderson p42, Getty Images/B2M Productions p24(A), Getty Images/Christine Balderas p66(D), Getty Images/Rob Blackburn p93(bl), Getty Images/Jeffrey Collidge p44(J), Getty Images/Michele Constantini p66(E), Getty Images/Datacraft Co Ltd p54(tl), Getty Images/Neil Emmerson p61(tr), Getty Images/Flying Colours Ltd p44(I), Getty Images/Ed Freeman p14(b), Getty Images/Juice Images p86(C), Getty Images/Brian Leatart p54(cmll), Getty Images/Frans Lemmans p26(b), Getty Images/Willie Malando p43(C), Getty Images/Geoff Masse p24(D), Getty Images/Kendall McMinimy p48(tr), Getty Images/MIXA p86(A), Getty Images/Marvin E. Newman p28(tl), Getty Images/Platform p92(B), Getty Images/Tony Robins p54(bcmll), Getty Images/Rubberball Productions p102, Getty Images/Joern Rymo p54(cl), Getty Images/David Sacks p6(D), Getty Images/Ian Schofield/iesphotography p8(tr), Getty Images/Joel Simon p78, Getty Images/Ariel Skelley p82(B), Getty Images/Siri Stafford p12(tr), Getty Images/STOCK4B Creative p61(cl), Getty Images/Jun Takashi p114(bcl), Getty Images/Ana Vianna p9(br); **Greenpeace** p99(tcr); **ICRC** p99(tr); **Image Source** pp8(bcr,cr,bl), 73(bmr,br); **Lonely Planet** Reproduced with permission from German Phrasebook & Dictionary © 2012 Lonely Planet pp66(C), 93(B), 117(B); **Macmillan Publishers Ltd**/Peter Day pp18(A-G), 65, 66(A); Macmillan Publishers Ltd/Rob Judges p88; Macmillan Publishers Ltd/David Tolley p36; **Milepost 92½** p26(C,D); **Photodisc** pp54(bml), 92(C); **Photoshot**/Xinhua p28(b); **Reuters**/David Gray pp97(C), 118(cl); **Rex Features**/Everett Collection pp6(B), 68(B), 89(br), Rex Features/© Paramount/courtesy Everett Collection p68(A), Rex Features/Warner Bros./courtesy Everett Collection p68(C), Rex Features/ITV p6(C), Rex Features/Nils Jorgensen p81(bmr), Rex Features/Theo Kingma p74(c), Rex Features/ David Magnus p84(cl), Rex Features/Ralph Metzger p81(cm,br), Rex Features/Brian Rasic p99(br), Rex Features/Sten Rosenlund p81(cr), Rex Features/Snap p6(A); **Save the Children** p99(cr); **Sony Computer Entertainment Europe Ltd** p44(E); **Peter Steiner** pp97(A), 118(tl); **Stockbyte** pp47(cr), 92(A), 93(E), 117(E); **Superstock** p9(bl); **Topfoto** pp34(cl), 97(B), 118(tcl); **Twitter** p38(tr).

Printed and bound in Spain

2017 2016 2015 2014 2013
10 9 8 7 6 5 4 3